"Fast-moving, almost lyrical in style, *What On Earth Are We Doing?* takes us into deep territory. I could not stop reading this book. The author found me, he understood me, and—best of all—he pointed me to the living Lord of truth, Jesus Christ."

REV. EARL F. PALMER
SENIOR PASTOR, UNIVERSITY PRESBYTERIAN CHURCH, SEATTLE, WA

"In his characteristic, stream-of-consciousness style, John Fischer explores the gap between the Church's growing consumer culture and the world at large.... John's advice is surprising, biblical, and relevant."

CHUCK SMITH, JR.
SENIOR PASTOR OF CAPO BEACH CALVARY CHAPEL
AUTHOR OF *ONE MINUTE MEDITATION*

"John Fischer shakes and rattles the unexamined Christian life.... He explores the habits and thought patterns of prevailing Christian cultures and arrives at a heartfelt celebration of the Gospels that eternally transcends them. His clarion call for a "Renaissance" is indeed a timeless summons for us all."

TERRY LINDVALL, PH.D.
PRESIDENT, REGENT UNIVERSITY

"One of our most powerful and provocative commentators makes his most important contribution to date.... John Fischer exposes the dangerous and damaging nature of the false secular/sacred dichotomy, and he gives us hope that thinking Christians can fight against it."

BOB BRINER
AUTHOR OF *ROARING LAMBS*

"*What On Earth Are We Doing* challenges us to engage the "secular" culture critically yet with love and humility, and demonstrates how it can be done. A fascinating, fresh, and thoroughly biblical proposal for relating to our society and culture."

DAVID WINTER
PRESIDENT, WESTMONT COLLEGE

What On Earth Are We Doing?

Finding Our Place
As Christians in the World

JOHN FISCHER

SERVANT PUBLICATIONS
ANN ARBOR, MICHIGAN

Vine Books is an imprint of Servant Publications especially designed to serve
evangelical Christians.

Published by Servant Publications
P.O. Box 8617
Ann Arbor, Michigan 48107

Cover design: Paul Higdon

97 98 99 00 10 9 8 7 6 5 4 3 2

Printed in the United States of America
ISBN 0-89283-976-7

LIBRARY OF CONGRESS CATALOGING-IN-PUBLICATION DATA

Fischer, John
    What on earth are we doing : finding our place as Christians in the world /
John Fischer.
        p.   cm.
    Includes bibliographical references.
    ISBN 0-89283-976-7
    1. Christianity and culture.   2. Church and the world.   3. Christian life.   I.
Title.
BR115.F57   1996
261—dc21   96-46559
                                                                    CIP

Love your enemies... and you will be sons of the Most High, because he is kind to the ungrateful and wicked. LUKE 6:35

Show proper respect to everyone: Love the brotherhood of believers, fear God, honor the king. 1 PETER 2:17

Contents

Introduction

Since the 1960s, the relevance of the gospel to contemporary culture has dominated the message of the church. First, it was important to make the gospel relevant to non-Christians so they might hear it and respond to it (e.g., the rock and roll music of the Jesus Movement). Then it was important to make the church relevant to the new, young Christians who were saved by the music so they would keep coming out on a Sunday morning to worship (e.g., the contemporary worship that now dominates many church services). Now, enterprising Christians create and market thousands of products and services to a Christian market eager to pay for a safer version of contemporary culture—a sort of decaffeinated world where Christians can have their Christianity and their culture, too.

This book is concerned about the emergence of a Christian subculture that encourages us to see ourselves as separate from the world not by beliefs and attitudes but by definable practices, identifiable markings, and cultural artifacts. The Oxford Encyclopedic English Dictionary defines culture as "the customs, civilization, and achievements of a particular time or people." I believe that Christ established the church (his body of believers on earth) not to develop its own separate customs, civilization, and achievements, but to infuse the customs, civilization, and achievements of every age and society with people who love and fear God. In opting to abandon the world for our own safer version of it, we are failing to deliver on this vital aspect of our presence in the world.

This book is primarily for Christians who are apprehensive about the growth of this Christian subculture in America and who wonder about their involvement in it. It is for Christians who have a keen interest in the world and yet have felt that interest stifled by a constricted worldview. And, it is a book for those who have a deep and lasting love for the gospel of Jesus Christ and feel concern for its ongoing representation in our generation.

ONE

Two Worlds

Is this vile world a friend of grace,
To help me on to God?[1]
ISAAC WATTS

1   Two Views

The Way We Think

In his book *The Christian Mind*, Harry Blamires states bluntly, "There is no longer a Christian mind."[2] By this he means that the mind which sees all of life as a perpetual act of worship under the canopy of God's grace, and embraces all learning as a study of his activity in the world, is nearly a thing of the past. Blamires suggests that between the ears of even the most well-meaning Christian, one will likely find a secular mind that thinks Christian thoughts from time to time.

In the course of a typical week, most Christians attend church, maybe a mid-week Bible study, and squeeze in a few moments for devotions. But by and large, we occupy our minds with the same pursuits and attitudes that fill any secular mind. If we could peer inside the mind of a Christian and a non-Christian as they work, read the newspaper, watch television, or drive along the expressway, we might see little difference between the two perspectives.

Most of us feel caught between two worlds, and we measure our dedication as Christians by how we balance the two. The more time spent doing Christian things, the more spiritual the person. And we tend to expect less spiritually from a person whose career demands a great deal of time in the world. In order for something "Christian" to occupy our minds, we have to be *doing* something "Christian" such as reading our Bibles or going to church or praying. And even when we pray, we have difficulty keeping the world at bay.

View 1: The Flight Attendant

On an airline flight not long ago, I was reading Blamires' book when a flight attendant came up to me, saw what I was reading, and launched into a sad tale about the conflict she was having between her job and her devotion to God. "I have been a Christian for two years," she said, "and I am so in love with the Lord that I want to spend more and more time with him and his Word. It's getting harder and harder for me to go to work. The other flight attendants only want to talk about boyfriends and affairs and shallow things. I hate this job because it takes me away from God."

Her devotion to the Lord is commendable, even enviable, and yet it presents a serious dilemma. For this flight attendant, God exists in a particular compartment of her life that she designates as spiritual. She is unable to think of him outside of that sphere because everything that has to do with her daily existence draws her away from God. Her job, and most likely many of the other things that take up her time, such as eating, shopping, cleaning house, balancing her checkbook, or any hobbies or sports are seen as secular activities God finds offensive or irrelevant. She sees him waiting for her, there in that quiet, holy place they share, to finish her necessary chores and secular diversions and get back to the spiritual reason for her life. She may even feel that most of life sullies her in some way, and she must tire of having to be alternately dirty and clean because of the soiled world she is forced to drag herself through every day.

I am reminded of Paul's word to the unmarried in 1 Corinthians 7, when he encourages singles to stay unmarried so they can be undistracted in their devotion to the Lord. "An unmarried woman or virgin is concerned about the Lord's affairs: Her aim is to be devoted to the Lord in both body and spirit. But a married woman is concerned about the affairs of this world—how she can please her husband. I am saying this for your own good, not to restrict you, but that you may live in a right way in undivided devotion to the Lord" (vv. 34-35). The flight attendant sees her job much like Paul saw marriage—necessary for many, but a deterrent to a total commitment.

This flight attendant is dealing with serious questions. Is the world a preclusion to faith? Is a person who deals daily with the stock market doomed to spiritual compromise, since "you cannot serve both God and Money" (Mt 6:24)? Is a pastor more spiritual than a businessman by nature of vocation alone?

The flight attendant's willingness to put her job on the line is evidence of an intense, radical faith. Don't we all often wonder if we are giving God enough of our time? If there are two separate worlds that Christians must balance, then this woman's world-view is truly consistent. To pass between worlds without blink-ing—to not even struggle over this apparent conflict—is more common. At least she is bothered by the conflict. How many Christians ignore this major dichotomy in their worldview?

View 2: The Swimsuit Model

Shortly after I talked with the flight attendant I happened upon another approach to the two-worlds dilemma. This was not a personal encounter, but an inadvertent viewing of a portion of the *Sports Illustrated* swimsuit edition video one night on HBO. *Sports Illustrated* produces an annual swimsuit edition to spice up the "down time" between the end of football season and the beginning of baseball. The issue is a bestseller, featuring beautiful, athletic female models displaying swimwear in exotic, outdoor settings. The racy swimsuits and provocative poses make this issue a big attraction among the magazine's primarily male readership. One would have to be more than naive to think that men were not getting anything more out of these pictures than the latest in female swimwear.

Few Christians would question the propriety of a subscription to *Sports Illustrated*, but once a year the envelope on sports gets pushed to the limits of soft porn. The video (even more provocative because it shows the models' movements that create the poses) is a documentary about the shooting of the photographs, commented on by the photographers and models, and narrated by the head of the modeling agency who lets the viewer in on some charming personal tidbits about the models' personal lives.

It was into this setting that one of these "girls" (as they are called in the show) decided to bring her Bible. Right before going on camera, she had a quiet moment on the beach with a book that no one knew was a Bible until a video camera came up over her bare shoulder and focused in on the words of the Gospel of John, chapter three. The narrator commented that this model was a deeply religious girl who reads her Bible and prays every day. A clip was then inserted where she shared a brief insight from her latest Bible study. And then, suddenly, she was laying her Bible down and posing on the beach as the photographer snapped away and the video camera zoomed in on her enticing moves.

Now for a guy like me, happening upon this program alone in a hotel room and immediately struggling on the borders of sin, this scene was a real shock. Why was she doing this? Was she trying to witness? Did she have misgivings about the morality of her work and figure that putting the Bible in the video would even the score—a kind of moral trade-off? Was she trying to catch her Christian brothers in the act of thinking they could get away with watching a little "Christian burlesque show"? As if to say, "I got you guys now. I have to do this for a living, but you don't have to watch! Hey, Fischer, is your wife with you?" Or, was she simply caught in the same trap as the flight attendant, between her job and her relationship to God—between two separate and distinct realms—and resolved to bring them both together by taking her Bible to work and having her devotions on the set?

Of course, I cannot answer for her, and can only address my reaction to what I saw. My guess is that she went to considerable trouble to get this "devotional moment" on camera. The narrator said she was their most popular model, and this would give her some negotiating power. She obviously wanted to make this statement and might have even insisted on it. Though this puzzling scene raises many questions, my purpose is not to address them here. I'm interested only in what this picture says to the rest of us.

As I watched her having her devotions in a setting that was far from devotional, it seemed to me that in her worldview, there was one world over here, and another world over there, and neither had anything to do with the other. Regardless of how much soul-searching went into the model's decision to be in this line of work, or how she processed her job and her faith, and acknowledging my own tendency to rush to judgment, I can only report that I saw an apparent lack of conflict. It looked as if she performed one of these tasks as easily as the other; and in that picture I think we can find something of the modern Christian mind that Harry Blamires was talking about. For it appears that the majority of Christians today who subscribe to a dualistic worldview have no problem moving from one realm to the other in a sort of spiritual schizophrenia. In this regard the swimsuit model is probably more in sync with contemporary Christianity than the flight attendant.

We too often bring our Christianity right up to the secular realm, but no further. We may read the Scriptures without letting them speak to the events, the motivations, the feelings, or priorities of our lives. We live in two worlds and each world has its own set of rules. That these rules are often in conflict doesn't matter, since they cover two distinctly different realms. What goes on in one has little to do with the other. The appeal of this dual worldview can be enticing to the nominal Christian. If God is not in both realms, then we can be secular without having to be spiritually conscious.

This works both ways. Rarely are we comfortable bringing the secular into the sacred realm to scrutinize it or allow it to reflect back on what is spiritual. Movies, art, economics, business ethics, politics, and critical thinking have little or no place in church, except when they have overtly spiritual applications or are a part of a particular subcultural agenda. Most of us keep God in his realm and the world in its realm and try to balance life between the two. As Harry Blamires has stated:

> We twentieth-century Christians have chosen the way of com-promise. We withdraw our Christian consciousness from the fields of public, commercial, and social life. When we enter these fields we are compelled to accept for purposes of discus-sion the secular frame of reference established there. We have no alternative except that of silence.... We have no Christian vocabulary to match the complexities of contemporary politi-cal, social, and industrial life. How should we have? A language is nurtured on usage, not on silence, however high-principled. And we have long since ceased to bring Christian judgment to bear upon the secular public world.[3]

The New Gnosticism

"Hear 'em both, hear 'em both... There's a pair for you. Always right. They couldn't have put it better."

"But we're saying just the opposite," said Lucy, stamping her foot with impatience.

"So you are, to be sure, so you are," said the Monopods. "Nothing like an opposite. Keep it up, both of you."[4]

In this scene from the *Chronicles of Narnia*, C.S. Lewis makes fun of our tendency to uncritically hold conflicting views. Such contradictory thinking is at least as old as the New Testament church. One of Christianity's earliest threats was Gnosticism, a blending of the gospel with certain philosophical theories held by a popular Greek sect, the members of which called themselves Gnostics, from the Greek word *gnosis* or knowledge. John wrote his first letter to the churches to refute a hybrid form of Christian Gnosticism.

Gnostic Christians believed that there was a distinct separation between the material and the spiritual worlds. The spiritual realm was the only one that mattered, since it was the seat of knowledge and contained the ultimate truth. The material world was an illusion and not to be trusted. Since the material world was not real, what you did in it was of no consequence. In practice, this boiled down to: Knowledge is everything. As long as you know the right things, you can do anything you want.

The Gnosticism of today is not much different: Believe the right things about God and do as you please. Christians don't actually admit to this as a life philosophy, of course, but it is what many of us do. We have been trained in the nuances of thinking with a split mind.

In the earliest part of this century evangelical theologians, then called fundamentalists, stood their ground for the preeminence of doctrinal knowledge. Biblical theology was under attack by liberal theologians and the need for orthodoxy in belief became paramount. All the attention was placed on *what* you believed. You were a Christian if you believed the right things: the inerrancy of

Scripture, the virgin birth, the deity and humanity of Christ, his death and resurrection in history, the resulting salvation for sinners through Christ's atonement for sin, the subsequent indwelling of the Holy Spirit in a believer's life, and the imminent return of Christ to judge the living and the dead. *Preaching* these things, *knowing* these things, *believing* these things was the issue. How you actually lived was defined as well, though most of the definitions were extrabiblical—abstaining from makeup, card-playing, theater-going, dancing, drinking, and smoking. This insured that there would be a marked difference in lifestyle between believers and unbelievers.

But since the '50s and the invasion of television and popular music into virtually every American home, popular culture has risen to a place of dominance in American life, and the extrabiblical marks of the Christian have slowly given way. Suddenly everyone's watching the same shows, listening to the same music, wearing the same clothes and makeup. Though my parents' generation of believers tried to stop this influence, it was useless. Christians were going to boogie one way or another, and the extrabiblical nature of these taboos sooner or later had to come to light.

In early 1996 Baylor University, the nation's largest Baptist institution, announced that it will allow dancing on campus for the first time in 151 years. "Dancing is just no longer an issue for 90 percent of people in Baptist life,"[5] said the president of the university in a *USA Today* article. Change the definitions. Redefine the borders. All it takes is a major respectable institution to come along and announce that dancing and Christianity are no longer in conflict, and a 151-year-old boundary suddenly vanishes as the university president and his wife take to the floor for the first waltz.

So what now? Now that we have lost one of the last vestiges of what made Christians different (i.e., real Christians don't dance), what is going to make us different? No wonder trustees of institutions such as Baylor University hang on to these taboos even long after it is clear that they are traditionally and not biblically based. Without cultural behavioral taboos, who will be able to tell the difference anymore between Christians and non-Christians? In cases such as this one where we face secular culture with a lack of Christian consciousness, the words of Harry Blamires again ring sadly true: "We have no alternative except that of silence."[6] While Christians are blindly embracing culture, few are offering intelligent biblical responses to that culture. As Christians become more and more worldly, we are becoming more and more uncertain as to what to do about our world and our apparent "worldliness."

So What's Different About Us?

The seeds of modern Gnosticism are blooming out of control in our evangelical garden, as Christians go on believing all the right things, but conform in so many ways to a culture that no one addresses. We have this vague memory of being different, but we're not sure anymore what's different about us. Preaching still emphasizes the fundamentals of the faith, but the practice of one's faith in society has never been a strong suit for evangelicals aside from a wholesale retreat from culture. Now we are in unfamiliar territory—many Christians are embracing culture, but don't know how to do this without losing faith. We're used to showing the world a manufactured model of how different we are. What will we say, now that we are so much the same?

Cultural taboos were popular because they provided us a watermark. No one had to think; everything was spelled out. Preachers could rail against these taboos from the pulpit, and congregations could be indignant about them from the pew without sacrifice to anyone's personal lives since no one wanted to take part in these things anyway. Now that most of these taboos have fallen, Christians are culturally floundering in a time when our lives have been shaped by popular cultural phenomena to an extent greater than ever before. By offering no practical means of melding popular phenomena into our everyday lives of faith, we are resigning ourselves to life in two separate worlds. And in those worlds, we are either torn between the two as the flight attendant was or, like the swimsuit model, we are seemingly oblivious to the fact that there is any conflict at all.

2   *A Third View*

A New Answer

But wait! There may yet be another way to address this two-world conflict without having to actually interact with our worldly culture as intelligent Christians. Forget all those two-world hassles; we can solve all these problems by creating our own world. For Christians trapped in cultural schizophrenia, there is an answer in the burgeoning Christian marketing subculture.

If you want to boogie, you can now boogie to Christian music. Do you like rap? Grunge? Heavy metal? Soft jazz? Alternative? Hard Rock? Psychedelic rock? You name it; we've got it. Want to be cool? Get a T-shirt, cap, or CD with a Christian message. Want to go to a concert and have your head blown away by an awesome display of lights and sound? Check *CCM* magazine because your favorite Christian artist is coming soon to a city near you. Looking for wholesome television entertainment free of violence and sex? Punch the family channel. Like MTV? Watch ZTV. Like talk radio? Listen to the best in Christian talk radio. Put the flight attendant on a Christian airplane. Let the model display clothes for discriminating Christian women in a Christian fashion magazine. This will work. And it's lucrative too!

Yes, the contemporary Christian subculture in America has already solved the conflict of two worlds by inventing an alternative in the form of a Christian world in every way as exciting as the secular one. Any twinge of doubt about accepting secular culture, any inkling of schizophrenic anxiety, can now be set aside by combining the best of both worlds. Christians can now reject the world and still keep what they liked best about it. Even better than having your cake and... (well, you know how it goes). The thinking was simple: provide alternative Christian entertainment for Christians and make money at the same time.

It didn't start this way. It began with the Jesus Movement of the early '70s and a sincere desire to reach the world for Christ through contemporary music. An explosion of new music soon reached the ears of a youth culture, spawning an entertainment industry tailor-made to the desires of new cultural Christians. But industry leaders could not resist the temptation to exploit this untapped new market. Even the rationale made sense: Christians are going to spend money on music and entertainment anyway, so they might as well spend it on music with a wholesome message, and keep the money in the Christian family. What could possibly be wrong with this?

There are a number of things wrong. For starters, the money doesn't stay in the Christian family. That's a myth. Some of the larger Christian publishing houses and record companies are now owned by secular corporations. Christian executives have to answer regularly to the bottom line. Many of the biggest investors in the Christian subculture do not have a sensitivity to ministry or to the things of God. Rather, they see the Christian subculture as an opportunity to seize upon a profitable new market.

The motive to provide wholesome entertainment with a message has met with limited success. Christian music has its greatest following among Christian kids who have been raised almost entirely inside the Christian subculture. They are being home-schooled or attend Christian schools and are in an environment where they have hardly heard any secular music. Those who have been exposed to secular music tend to find Christian music unrealistic. When you listen to non-Christians asking hard questions in their music about a real world in decline, and then you listen to Christian music about a naive and happy world where everything is going to be all right, you have to close your eyes to buy the Christian package. It is not that Christianity is incapable of grappling with the deep, dark questions of our culture; it's just that no one, secure and happy on the inside of a subculture, wants to. Christians have always desired heaven too soon. And a positive Christian artist, sweetly smiling and singing about hope, is simply not going to connect with a kid who has already connected with Pearl Jam, Nirvana, and Nine Inch Nails, groups that look at the world darkly and capture their own loneliness, fear, and alienation in their music. Most Christian artists are not addressing the real feelings of a lost generation.

Across the Great Divide

The greatest danger of a Christian subculture, however, is that it subverts the reason God has placed us in the world. The more ingrown we become, the less we have to contribute to the world around us. We are already dangerously close to being irrelevant. Studs Terkel foreshadowed the growing social, ethnic, and religious divisions in our society in his book *The Great Divide,* and the Christian subculture is making that divide come true.

Take, for instance, the growing market for Christian fiction. More and more shelves in Christian bookstores are stocked with fiction, and most of the large secular superstores now have inspirational fiction sections featuring popular Christian writers. But what kind of fiction is this? Is it like the great psychological dramas of Dostoevski, grappling with morality and justice—novels that give us windows on our own struggles and compromises with sin? Is it fiction like the allegories of C.S. Lewis, carrying deep theological truths across the great divide to a culture that will accept in a story a message it might reject in any other form? Is it fiction like the novels of Frederick Buechner, weaving faith into the doubts and complexities of human existence? Is it fiction that can lead us back into our world with greater insight and courage?

How about letting one of Christian fiction's most popular writers answer the question. Francine Rivers was the author of 3.5 million copies of secular romance novels before converting to Christianity and "inspirational" romance writing. As she tells it, she used to write about men, women, and sex, but now she writes about "men, women, and God."[7] "It's Christianity Lite," admits one Christian book dealer. "They want books with family values that are fast, funny, and not too preachy."[8] In other words, these are books that only someone tucked away in a Christian subculture would want to read. Who wants to take on the complex issues of a postmodern society and risk starvation, trying to get their story across the great divide, when they can be hugely successful on the Christian side writing fast, funny, not-too-preachy stories about family values for a subculture that doesn't want to cross anything?

It's tragic that we are expending so much energy creating and marketing for the Christian subculture, when a good story is one of the most important ways we have of reaching a postmodern age that is closed to absolute truth. Such a tragedy illustrates how living in a Christian culture removes our voice from the world. It's as if we're holding a private party. Of course, we justify our private parties—our concerts and dramatic productions—by inviting the world to them, but who in the world wants to come? Why would the world be interested in what seems nothing but a copy of what they already have? And anyway, didn't Jesus send us into the world? I seem to remember that he went to *their* parties.

Nowhere in the New Testament is there any call to believers to form a separate culture from the world. We were called to be separate from the world, but never to leave. Some Christians confuse 2 Corinthians 6:17 as a call to leave the world. "Therefore come out from them and be separate, says the Lord. Touch no unclean thing." This section, however, concludes, "Since we have these promises, dear friends, let us purify ourselves from everything that contaminates body and spirit, perfecting holiness out of reverence for God" (7:1). Paul is talking about an internal, personal holiness, not a separate culture he wants us to create, as if living in it will make us holy by osmosis.

The call is to go out into the world, and we keep hoping that this "Christian" subculture we have created will somehow go for us, through its growing power and influence. But in forming our own culture, all we have done is to leave the world without a witness from the inside, where we are supposed to be.

Ring Around the Christian

During the height of the Jesus Movement, someone came up with the idea for a Christian Yellow Pages, to give the body of Christ easy access to all the businesses in an area owned or operated by Christians. I can remember thinking what a good idea this was. Keep the business in the family. It was during the early '70s when I first heard of this, when the church was fired up, lay people were finding ministries and getting excited about their faith, and Christian music was in its fledgling years. No one was even thinking about careers yet, much less a subculture. Radio and television were waiting in the wings for the Christian message. Suggestions of a "Christian" *this* and a "Christian" *that* in contemporary culture were everywhere. It seemed as if we all had answered the same phone call from God.

I ran into two young Christian entrepreneurs at the time who were excited about their new business of designing greeting cards. Caught up in the thinking of the day, I asked them if their cards were Christian cards. They replied, "Well, they aren't all saved, but we pray for them every day." That was when I first started to wonder about the way we were using the word "Christian."

In these twenty-five years, the word *Christian* has been altered. It once was a noun—meaning a person whose life was turned over to Christ. Slowly it began to find new usage as an adjective, identifying a host of things from the secular culture that had been given a Christian version. One has only to serpentine the aisles of the annual Christian Booksellers Association convention to experience four football fields of "Christian" (*adj.*) stuff. In the words of my card-designer friends, I'm not sure all this stuff is saved or, more importantly, that it has helped us save the world. What does the world think about all this Christian merchandise? What message is the world getting today through the publicity the Christian subculture is now enjoying? How has all this "Christian stuff" helped us relate to the non-Christian world around us? Has it made us more vulnerable? More compassionate? More eager to share our faith?

Little did we know what would transpire in twenty years! The Christian Yellow Pages was nothing compared to the multibillion dollar industry that has developed around Christian products and services, the sum of which can potentially replace the secular world for Christians. Nor did anyone realize the network that would develop through Christian radio and direct mail marketing, binding together a force for political power that can link up with other conservative organizations and mobilize a grassroots coalition of voters with a moral agenda. These events have drastically changed the shape of the world as Christians know it. No longer threatened by a secular culture immediately outside their door, millions of contemporary Christians now have a buffer zone—a cultural ring around themselves. "Christians today... naively assume that because they are so involved in church and the evangelical subculture, with its own music, arts, events, conferences, books, and broadcasting, that they are sailing safely past the isle of the Sirens."[9]

Protected by this buffer zone, our desire to interact with the world has diminished as has the need to give an answer for our hope to unbelievers. For many, the only time spent outside the buffer zone is when we are at work or at the local shopping mall. We minimize the need to speak for ourselves in matters of faith and culture by making our home away from the arena where a cultural debate could even take place. Also, we feel little need to prepare to debate our faith, when a collective voice speaks for everyone—even a coalition to suggest how we should vote. Personal encounter with the lost is almost nonexistent, since Christians caught up in the subculture know few non-Christians personally. All this disengagement with the world makes it difficult to maintain a heart of compassion toward unbelievers.

3   *Conclusion*

Your God Is Too Small

Are these our only options—to live in two worlds in either frustration or cultural schizophrenia, or to remain insulated in the small safe zone that rings us with a Christian subculture? In the first, Christianity fills only a portion of a believer's existence; in the second, it may take up more of one's life, but reality is reduced to that which can carry the "Christian" label. Suddenly I hear again the classic book by J.B. Phillips that has accomplished more with its title than some books have done with their entire contents: *Your God Is Too Small.*

Our God is too small if he exists in only a portion of our existence. Our God is too small if we need a Christian label before we can even locate him. Our God is too small if we believe he inhabits a world smaller than the whole world as we know it. We are right that our time spent with God is vital; it's just that our God is too small to fill up all of our time. We have difficulty seeing him as interested in our everyday lives.

How did we begin to worship such a culturally anemic God, and how do we find our way out? Does our Christianity have anything to do with how we spend our time, how we entertain ourselves, how we work, how we play, how we vote, how we buy and sell, and how we participate in the world around us?

In *The Scandal of the Evangelical Mind,* Mark Noll laments the way Christians have failed to pursue

what it means to think like a Christian about the nature and workings of the physical world, the character of human social structures like government and the economy, the meaning of the past, the nature of artistic creation, and the circumstances attending our perception of the world outside ourselves. Failure to exercise the mind for Christ in these areas has become acute in the twentieth century.[10]

Our confusion about the world and our place in it begins with how we think about the world and our place in it. Since we are products of our culture as well as of our faith, we must be prepared to look in both directions for the major influences on the current Christian mind. What shapes our thinking as Americans? And, what shapes our thinking as American *Christians?* It is to these influences that I now wish to turn our attention.

Two

Thinking Someone Else's Thoughts

"Hey lads! We're visible again."

"Visible we are," said one in a tasseled red cap who was obviously the Chief Monopod. "And what I say is, when chaps are visible, why they can see one another."

"Ah, there it is, there it is, Chief," cried all the others. "There's the point. No one's got a clearer head than you. You couldn't have made it plainer."[1]

C.S. LEWIS

1   *The Thinking Christian*

Beyond Understanding

History has produced a number of notable thinking Christians, people like Saint Augustine, Thomas Aquinas, Blaise Pascal, Martin Luther, C.S. Lewis, Dorothy Sayers, and Francis Schaeffer, who are known not only for their religious convictions but also for writings that present the Christian faith as a rational belief.

But to many today, the term "thinking Christian" seems an oxymoron. If thinking and Christianity ever were compatible, they have had a falling out of late. Belief now is often equated with blind acceptance of truth as it is spelled out by whatever spiritual authority a person or group recognizes. Dutiful followers sit in rapt attention before magnetic personalities who dish out the goods for hungry souls. Heads nod, hands clap, and minds behave like washing machines on soak cycle.

Anyone who has ever watched Christian television has probably seen it—whatever a speaker says is received with unquestioning assent, as the heads nod up and down. The people are taking it straight, like strong "gospel truth" medicine from a trusted doctor.

Questioning in such an environment can be taken as rebellion and disbelief. There seems to be no precedent for thinking something through as a natural step toward the ownership of an idea. Many people don't bring minds to church to engage in learning more about God; they bring heads that need only to be filled.

I grew up in a strong evangelical church, and my parents put me through every form of Christian education available at the time: Sunday school, Christian Endeavor, Vacation Bible School, and annual summer and winter camps. And yet, it was not until I was in a freshman Introduction to Philosophy class at Wheaton College that it dawned on me that my Christian faith and my mind could actually serve each other well. With what joy I discovered the writings of C.S. Lewis and Blaise Pascal! With what excitement I learned that contemporary evangelical thinkers such as Francis Schaeffer and Os Guinness were trying to put the Christian faith in context with the history of thought and reason as well as with the daily newspaper! That this news came as a surprise to me says something about the messages conveyed during my childhood.

However subtle and perhaps even unintended, those messages made me assume my mind was suspect and any questions I had sprang from a rebellious spirit or a disbelieving heart. Belief was supposed to be simple; thinking was complicated. Those with strong faith learned to shut their minds and simply believe. The faith message of my Christian upbringing was, "Thinking too much might lead you to doubt, skepticism, or unbelief."

At the root of such fear is an assumption that too much thinking will inevitably lead to an unanswerable question—a black hole in our faith through which we might fall into some bottomless pit. In fact, the opposite is true. The unanswerable question is the reason we *must* believe. A God who fills up what we don't understand is a God worthy of worship. A god who answers everything in a three-ring binder is not an object of worship. It's a seminar to attend.

When Samson's parents encountered a man who prophesied about their son, they inquired of him concerning his name, not knowing that he was an angel of the Lord. He replied, "Why do you ask my name? It is beyond understanding" (Jgs 13:18). They then proceeded to watch in amazement and horror as the man/angel ascended into heaven in the dancing fingers of their flaming sacrifice to God. When our minds fail us with God, it is not because of a lack of faith or a spirit of rebellion, but because we have met what Manoah and his wife met—that which is beyond our understanding.

New Christians are often taught to trust uncritically the sources that brought them the good news of Christ. For those reared in a Christian environment, the mind is often presented as an untrustworthy friend, more eager to respond to secular impulses than sacred ones. When the mind is discounted as a useful tool, Christians are encouraged not to think for themselves.

Have you ever been in a group of believers when someone asked a question that didn't have an easy answer? Disapproving glances were probably thrown at the questioner as if to say, "Don't you know we don't ask such questions here?" There is a tacit understanding within many churches and fellowship groups that this gospel ship navigates best if you don't rock the boat.

Not having to think for ourselves in areas of faith frees us from the responsibility to integrate our faith with the world around us. A system which allows us to believe without thinking also allows us to sin without thinking, be entertained without thinking, vote without thinking, and generally follow the bent of the group.

2   *An Age of Professionals*

Someone's Thinking, Somewhere...

This lack of critical thinking is not exclusive to Christians. It is rampant in a culture that stands by and watches as its foundations of truth and learning daily capitulate to the gods of specialization and pragmatism. Many people concern themselves mainly with knowledge that is useful to them in a specialized field and, ultimately, a vocation. Like so many other areas of our culture, knowledge is more and more dominated by economics. It is necessary to learn only what one needs to know to get by—or to get ahead.

We live in an age of specialization where somebody, somewhere, knows everything there is to know about any given thing. No one could possibly be an expert on everything, but rest assured that everything has its expert. For this reason, few of us feel the necessity of bothering to know much beyond what we absolutely have to know for our immediate concerns. The rest we leave to others.

You can see this specialization manifested in almost any area of our culture. When I was in high school, athletes often lettered in as many as four sports. Though this may still be true in rural towns, in metropolitan areas athletic students usually specialize in only one sport. Only rarely do they attempt two unless they happen to be Bo Jackson or Deion Sanders. Individual sports teams practice year round now, not just during their season. Competition demands it. High school sports are farm clubs for college, which many are cutting short to join the pros. You can hardly go out for a sport anymore just for the fun of it.

My son Christopher recently tried out for soccer at his high school, and failed to make the team. Nothing unusual about that until you consider he's been playing with American Youth Soccer Organization teams (A.Y.S.O.) since he was old enough to bunch together with fifteen other little tykes and wait for the ball to squirt out. Everyone who made the high school team, however, had been playing on club soccer teams for at least two years, a much more rigorous and demanding approach to the game.

Christopher simply could not compete on the same level as kids who had devoted the better part of their last few years to soccer, even though he is one of the better A.Y.S.O. players, and has made their all-star team two years in a row.

This same kind of specialization can be seen across all levels of society today—in the workplace, in technology, in the medical field, in education. Os Guinness calls it the "PhD-ing" of our services and institutions. Every human problem must be solved first by a study of experts who advance no further than the paper their reports are printed on. This worship of expertise is disabling society and proliferating schools that keep people dumb, a penal system that is counterproductive, and a legal system that merely lines the pockets of lawyers.[2]

Christopher is finishing his junior year in high school, and we are just now beginning to stare down that long list of procedures that make up the college application process. This system has produced such a highly competitive scramble for acceptance that there are now independent private counselors who, for a generous fee, will help the prospective college student through the maze of college selection, testing, application process, and financial aid—a service high school counseling departments once provided free of charge. It now takes a specialist to help you get into the right college, and every day our mailbox is full of materials from companies who provide these services. With all these counseling services vying for our money, Christopher suggested that we need a specialist to help us select the right specialist.

With all this specialization in our society, why shouldn't it also show up in the church? Why shouldn't we be glad that someone, somewhere, is an expert on faith? If somebody, somewhere is doing all the necessary thinking about being a Christian in today's society, then the average believer doesn't need a personal apologetic for his or her faith in our pluralistic world.

Robert W. Jenson, professor of religion at St. Olaf College in Minnesota, is worried that even pastors are no longer doing the deep theological thinking required to keep the church on track, because theologians now specialize in such things. "In the ancient church," he says, "the theologians were the pastors of congregations." Today, he points out, theologians teach in seminaries, and pastors are busy with administration and counseling—tasks that professional therapists and businessmen in the congregation are much more qualified to do. Jenson concludes, "A pastor who is not a theologian is really quite a useless entity."[3]

But wait. Maybe there is a lesson here for the rest of us, too. Couldn't this same pithy statement—"a useless entity"—apply equally as well to those of us who have handed over the task of faith-thinking to someone else?

Pastors, priests, and theologians get paid to do religion on our behalf. Christian publishers exist to provide resources with answers to difficult questions. Somewhere there is a book or a video or an article about whatever confuses you. Check it out. No—don't even bother. Just know that it's there. As long as someone, somewhere, did the required thinking, you can take their word for it.

Just Enough to Get By...

It's understandable that many people feel overwhelmed by the wealth of information available to us today. The rapid advances in computer technology at the end of the twentieth century offer us countless choices. The world is now a supermarket of information, but access to all this information doesn't mean we know what to do with it. We purchase a computer and wonder if we know even 5 percent of what it can do. We jump on the Internet and feel as if we are sticking one toe in an ocean. And yet somebody programmed our computer with the software necessary to use it. Somebody, somewhere, knows how it all works. It isn't necessary for any one of us to know everything—it's impossible. We need to know only enough to get by. This is the way of survival in the 1990s.

"All the news that's fit to print" is printed on the front page of every issue of *The New York Times*. "All the news that's fit to print" is more than we'll ever read. So what do we read? Just enough to get by, or we cancel our subscription to the *Times* and watch the six o'clock news, or forget the news altogether.

A myriad of choices confronts the average American every day—choices of consumer products, clothes, music, movies, recreation, television channels, and food. In each category quality ranges from the discount mega-store to the connoisseur boutique, from Wal-Mart to Starbucks. It's enough to stagger the mind. Just try ordering a cup of coffee these days and notice what you're up against. Whole bean? Ground? Espresso? Latte? Cappuccino? Mocha? Decaffeinated? Regular? Cream? Soy milk? Sugar? Sweetener? It's enough to overwhelm anyone.

It is just as easy to be overwhelmed in the area of faith. Have you ever felt so confused by the myriad of spiritual points of view that instead of considering the validity of any one of them, you end up walking away, like walking away from a shopping mall, suddenly convinced that old sweater you've been wearing will suit you just fine for a few more months?

Few of us feel personally responsible to articulate our faith even in church, much less in the marketplace. After all, the church is run by specialists. They, along with the writers of more books than anyone will ever read, are the spiritual somebodies who have this thing down pat. Leave it to them to grapple with the mysteries and ambiguities of faith. If we just go to church, we can all manage well enough.

3   *America the Practical*

What Works Is True

In his introduction to a conversation on the Mars Hill Tapes with John Patrick Diggins, author of the book *The Promise of Pragmatism*, Ken Myers states, "The task of trying to understand the dynamics of contemporary culture often leads us back to ideas, thinkers, movements, and fads that have deep and long-forgotten roots but which continue to bear fresh and sometimes troubling fruit."[4] He then introduces us to what he calls America's most important philosophical tradition—the philosophy of pragmatism.

Reading about the origins of pragmatism is a bit like finding out about a forebear you didn't know very well. My wife recently received an informative article about her grandfather who died when she was young. Turns out he was a very influential banker who steered a fledgling savings and loan company successfully through the Great Depression and turned it into the largest bank in Rochester, New York. His creative business ideas, high level of self-motivation, and networking in the community are all evidenced and blooming profusely today in his granddaughter. Now I know where she got it. In the same way, we might learn something about ourselves by investigating where our bent towards the practical has come from.

Over several generations, pragmatic thinking has become as American as apple pie. Though some elements of pragmatism are enjoying a mild "renaissance" among neopragmatists such as Richard Rorty, Stanley Fish, and Cornel West,[5] it is not discussed much as a serious philosophy anymore, as it was in the early part of the twentieth century. And yet, pragmatism doesn't need to be discussed for its influence to be felt. The *Encyclopedia of Philosophy* states, "To have disappeared as a special thesis by becoming infused in the normal and habitual practices of intelligent inquiry and conduct is surely the pragmatic value of pragmatism."[6]

Pragmatism, the only tradition of serious philosophical thought that can carry the label "Made in America," has lost much of its original intent. That pragmatic thinking should actually end up keeping people from thinking and exploring is quite the opposite of what its originators intended—to create a philosophy of truth based on the usefulness of thoughts and ideas. Theirs was a reaction against a tradition of European thinkers and armchair philosophers who, by American standards, sat around contemplating the naval of truth without giving truth any practical relevance. The burgeoning American spirit of individualism and free enterprise at the end of the nineteenth century was looking for a philosophical taproot and found it in the intellectual pursuits of three main thinkers, Charles Sanders Peirce (1838-1914), William James (1842-1910), and John Dewey (1859-1952).

Charles Sanders Peirce first proposed the basic ideas of pragmatism in 1878, in a series of essays in which he defined belief as a rule of action. Doubt was the opposite of belief, and the purpose of thinking or inquiry was the elimination of doubt so that one could arrive at a settled belief.

In 1898, William James popularized Peirce's theories and asserted that the practical experiences due to the consequences of ideas were more concrete than the ideas themselves. Indeed, James would hold that different ideas that resulted in the same consequences in practice were really the same idea in different words. The only criteria for truth is that it works in practice. Or, stated in its simplest form: What works is true. And the Great American Principle was born.

John Dewey, an admirer of Charles Darwin's theory of evolution, then took pragmatism one step further. He acknowledged that what works would have to change as society evolved, and proposed that our minds were instruments that could direct the course of social evolution and reshape our environment. Dewey was a philosopher for the common man. He believed that philosophy is useful only as it deals with specific problems of all human beings. True ideas are those that work best for attaining common human goals.

No philosophy has affected American life and thinking more than pragmatism. With its basic optimism, its emphasis on action, and its belief in a future that can be shaped by human ideas and efforts, pragmatism has wedded itself to American individualism in an almost unbreakable bond. Pragmatism embodies, more than any other philosophy or ideology, what is unique to the essential American character.[7]

But pragmatism was also a response to a gathering loneliness that the theories of Charles Darwin left behind in a once God-centered universe. All three of these men were profoundly influenced by Darwin's thinking, and perhaps were unprepared for the loss of authority that the theory of evolution left in its wake. Pragmatism seemed an answer to a universe that had lost its Guiding Hand. Truth, no longer accessible by belief, could now be decided by practice. Understanding the universe, and thus understanding the God behind it, was no longer the paradigm. Darwin left humanity alone to develop on its own, and pragmatism would provide a new paradigm for coping and adjusting to the world. Rather than understanding a God-centered universe as Renaissance thinkers had once tried to do, we would now have to figure out our way in a man-centered world.

Thus, pragmatism has come to be known as a philosophy of

expedience. Theories mean nothing until they can be verified through one's experience. What works is true, and by "working" pragmatists mean that which is useful and beneficial to individuals (Peirce and James) or to society (Dewey). To determine the meaning or truth of ideas, one must evaluate their "practical consequences," "usefulness," "workability." One can immediately see how tailor-made these ideas became to the Carnegies, the Rockefellers, and the Henry Fords of America. What a boon to a growing capitalistic society! William James even coined the term "cash value" to express the usefulness of an idea. Though he would not have meant for this term to have the crass materialistic meaning that "cash value" has for us today, the seeds of this modern exploitation were planted.

Emerging from Puritan backgrounds that included the teachings of Jonathan Edwards and a fascination with the religious philosophy of Pascal, James' philosophy was the most religious of the three pragmatists. He argued that belief was beneficial to those who believed, not in a self-serving way, but as intellectually satisfying. It was not only good to believe; one *ought* to believe. But in the end, no matter how convincing the argument, belief still came down to one's experience. Justification for religious beliefs became a purely subjective matter and not an objective truth about a God who exists outside of any human experience of him.

Pragmatism is all about results. Its engine is problem-solving. Doubt is the opposite of belief, and the purpose of thinking or inquiry is the elimination of doubt so one can arrive at a settled belief. And belief is proven by the good it does the believer. Thus was born the rationale behind the idea that believing in God is not a requirement from the nature of God, but is valuable in that it benefits us. In this way the pragmatists framed religious discussion in the same terms as their search for truth. Belief was important only insofar as it benefited the believer. Pragmatists would not be so bold as to put it in these words, but what they really meant was: God does not exist unless I find, by believing in him, something that benefits me.

Herein lie the greatest dangers of pragmatism: its evolutionary conception of truth and its elevation of the experience of the individual as the final interpreter of truth. To the pragmatists, truth is not a fixed property. In James' own words, "Truth *happens* to an idea. It *becomes* true, is *made* true by events."[8]

The only way we know something is true is by verifying it in our experience. Thus, the step from pragmatism's concept of truth, "becoming true," to the postmodern notion of truth being what is "true for me" is indeed a very small one. They are, in fact, two ways of saying the same thing. Peirce, James, and Dewey would be surprisingly at home among many of today's post-modern thinkers.[9]

The American Idea of Success

Did America invent pragmatism or did pragmatists invent America? Like two people who have been married for so long you can hardly distinguish one from the other, pragmatism and American ideals have become almost inseparable. Here's a case in point. For the last two days, there has been a full-page advertisement in *The Los Angeles Times* for a major business seminar on success. "How much you earn is determined by how much you learn," is the subtitle. The seminar features eight well-known speakers addressing such topics as: "Using Goals to Chart Your Course of Action," "How to Dominate Your Circumstances," "The Five Keys to Failure and How to Eliminate Them," "How to Be Happy While You're Getting Rich," "The Opportunities That Make America Great," and "The Secrets of Living Life to Its Fullest." According to the ad, "This is your best opportunity to sit down with the experts and develop a plan to optimize your success. Gain the latest secrets of success *that work* in today's world."

Peirce, James, and Dewey would be proud to know their philosophies are having such an effect on businesspeople today. I doubt that William James would rejoice at seeing "cash value" taken so literally. According to this advertisement, eight famous people about to descend on the Anaheim Pond will eliminate all doubt by revealing the truth that has been proven true by their experience. This truth is made even more self-evident by the fact that the seminar itself is *already* a success, being held in a 14,000-seat auditorium for the fourth straight year.

Yet, there are deeper questions that seminars such as these will never address. Is success measured only by money and power? Is the rich man in a limousine always happier than the homeless man he passes on the street? Are we able to dominate all our circumstances? Can we change our world for the better? If Americans have been operating on this philosophy for so long, why is our country in such a mess today? Though these questions may enter the minds of skeptics, this seminar does not have to answer or even address them because it is based on "truth" as defined by the pragmatists: that is, the notion that what works is true. The truth of this seminar is self-evident. It is true because it is working and people are cashing in on its benefits.

But what if what works in the practical world doesn't tell the whole truth? What if what works is morally wrong, leaving a path of destruction in its wake? What if the speakers for this conference have manipulated success? What if God has not designed everyone to be rich? What if the great American dream is possible only for a few and not available to all of the 14,000 people who sign up for this seminar at $49 a pop? The pragmatic mind does not entertain these questions. The pragmatist recognizes only that these speakers are obviously successful. Their principles work;

therefore, they must be true since what is true is what works; so plop down your $49 and obtain similar results. This thinking is so obvious to the American mind that it seems redundant to spell it out and almost sacrilegious to question it.

4   *Christian Pragmatism*

Faith That Works

We know that what is true doesn't necessarily "work," at least by popular definition. Ask Job, ask the martyrs, ask Paul in prison, ask Christ on the cross if believing God "works" and you are likely to get a different answer.

Nevertheless, pragmatic thinking has a strong grip on Christianity in America, just as it does on secular America. Hundreds of unknown pastors regularly attend growth conferences held by famous colleagues who are obviously successful, judging by the numbers of people in their congregations. Whatever they are doing is working and, therefore, is tantamount to truth, for the same reason the success seminar is true. But is it biblical? That's a question that may or may not be addressed at the conferences; and even if it is, the biblical truth will probably not stand up as convincingly as the practical one. The Bible doesn't fare very well in America when it goes against what works. It is usually reinterpreted to agree with the practical, or is ignored altogether. We are brazen enough these days to bow to the pragmatic idol of success, even with God in the same room.

Pragmatism's grip on Christian thought is evidenced as well by the titles of many Christian books that begin like the topics of a success seminar:

"How to..."

"The Five Keys to..."

"The Secrets of..."

"The Primary Tools of..."

"A Step-by-Step Blueprint for..."

"Five Quick, Easy Ways to..."

and so on. As Christians, we are just as eager to improve our lives as non-Christians. There's an assumption that if faith doesn't work, no one will want it. According to the great American philosophy, if faith doesn't work, it isn't true.

Pooh-Speak

An insightful article in *Christianity Today*, November 1992, delved into the relationship of pragmatism and contemporary Christianity. The author, Rodney Clapp, chose a most unusual purveyor of current pragmatism, in the much loved children's character Winnie-the-Pooh. Pooh, "a noted Western philosopher," is sitting on a log when he hears a buzzing sound and deduces that it must be a bee. The only reason for being a bee, according to Pooh, is to make honey for Pooh's own enjoyment.

This incident shows Pooh to be a pragmatic individualist. He cannot imagine the bees possessing an existence and purpose apart from his own use and interest.... Pooh is the quintessential consumer, entirely practical and entirely self-centered: The only reason for being a bee is to make honey and the "only reason for making honey is so I can eat it."

Thus reasoning... Pooh has a range of other possibilities blocked from his vision. He cannot see, for instance, the wider ecological purpose of bees, how they weave into the fabric of flora and fauna not only by providing honey, but also by such crafts as pollinating flowers. Another thing Pooh cannot see is a theological purpose for bees: that in the wonder of their existence, they speak and spell the glory of a Creator God.[10]

Clapp discusses the questionable nature of a truth that uses experience as its only verification, and goes on to point out that pragmatic language dominates our God-talk. Sooner or later the Christian pragmatist has to face the question: "Is holiness good for you?" Clapp would say the answer is irrelevant. "God's holiness is not for my use or self-interest." In other words, God's holiness and my experience are on two different planes. You cannot judge one by the other.

In selecting Winnie-the-Pooh as the pragmatist, Clapp has captured the seeming harmlessness of these philosophies which makes them even more dangerous. Pragmatic truth may validate my experience and limit my vision at the same time. Pooh's reasoning is true and verifiable for him, but grossly incomplete in the wider scope of things. Pragmatism represses deeper thinking because it stops with what is useful to me. If I can resolve my doubts, then there are no more doubts to resolve. If I have no questions on a topic, then there must be no more questions to ask.

The average Christian in America exhibits a strange brew of pragmatic ideology and biblical belief. Like Peirce, most American Christians believe that doubt is the opposite of belief. The goal of a Christian mind is to eliminate all doubt and arrive at a settled place. Once there, such a mind is closed to further inquiry, since to question would mean to doubt. This is why Christians are often perceived as having closed minds. When we talk and act as if an issue is already settled by the Bible, even if we may not know exactly *how* the Bible settles it, we are not open to discussing it. Somebody, somewhere, knows what the Bible says. This is how

Christians can claim, "I don't know about such and such, I just stand on the Word of God," and close the issue without ever thinking critically about it or what the Word of God actually says.

And yet like the pragmatists, we live as if Christianity were true, not because it is true, but because it *works* for us. The bees make honey only for us to eat. Thus as Christians, we are constantly trying to prove that we are happier, healthier, more loving, more successful, and have better overall lives than those who aren't Christians. Many evangelistic appeals are made on the basis of what Christianity offers, not because we all are sinners in need of salvation. Pulpits and radio talk shows give practical advice to improve our lives so that we will not lag behind the world. If Christians are not successful, then Christianity can't be true, at least according to the ideas of our great grandfather Pragmatism.

Even the newfound political clout Christians are enjoying in America has pragmatic underpinnings. And as we approach the end of the twentieth century, we see Christians involved in the political process in unprecedented numbers. They believe our voice can make a moral difference in society. Some even believe we can bring a spiritual kingdom to America through a political process. We are flexing powerful political muscles right now, and the power to effect a practical change in society is intoxicating stuff to the pragmatic mind.

Inquiring Minds Inquire No More

The danger of pragmatic Christianity is that it limits the mind to the practical. Truth is reduced to what works. The pragmatic Christian mind does not even try to reach beyond what it can grasp. We don't need to have inquiring minds or the patience to contemplate and explore our world—we are too busy explaining everything. Instead of inquiring into God's vast universe, our minds are already made up. There are no open ends. Instead of pulling up the planks of a platform of ideas to see what is underneath, historically and biblically, pragmatic Christians want all their ideas nailed down.

Mystery, wonder, and true worship are largely absent today. Christianity should *start* people thinking; but instead, pragmatic Christianity *stops* people from thinking and encourages them to accept what has already been determined. Instead of engaging in exploratory thought—roaming around in large fields of doubt, paradox, and ambiguity—Christians rush to the elimination of questioning and doubt as the highest truth, and to the effecting of political change in society as the highest good. The idea that one can believe and doubt at the same time is not only unthinkable; it is also viewed as un-American in light of our pragmatic forefathers who saw belief as the opposite of doubt.

Delving into the mysteries of God seems a waste to the pragmatic mind. The pragmatic Christian does not care to rummage around in the great intellectual attic of truth. He is not comfortable with paradox and wants explanations; and yet, God and his truth cannot be contained in the human mind. Blaise Pascal wrote, "The knowledge of God is very far from the love of Him,"[11] meaning that the more you try to make God make sense to you, the further away from him you have to go. To be close to God is to be close to the mystery of that which cannot be known or solved or put into practical terms. This kind of pursuit only frustrates the pragmatic mind that finds it hard to grasp the usefulness of worshiping that which cannot be known.

In his Bell Lectures, Robert Farrar Capon captured the paradox of the gospel in a truly fetching manner:

The Gospel proclaims a disreputable salvation. It hands us neither an intellectually respectable God nor a morally serious one. It gives us an action of God in Christ that is foolishness to the Greek in us and a scandal to our Jewishness. It presents us with a Sabbath-breaking Messiah whose supreme act is to be executed as a criminal—and who then rises and disappears, leaving us with a blithe assurance that everything is repaired even though, as far as we can see, nothing has been fixed at all.[12]

In these last few decades, the church has had far greater success solving people's problems than it has leading them to drink at the fountain of any great paradox. In churches that are booming, the sermons are practical and relevant to current needs. But in spelling faith out in such practical terms, are they not running the risk of driving people farther away from the love of God? The inquisitive nature of faith is easily lost in the practice of principles. Remember, as the pragmatist sees it, bees make honey for him to eat, not for him to observe and wonder at how such a thing could be.

The Book of Job does not have much to offer Christians geared toward the practical, unless all the pain, suffering, and loss Job went through is a means of gaining back double. This did happen to him, but is never mentioned as being connected to his pain. Job's suffering led him closer to a God he could not comprehend—a God who shut Job's mouth and stopped all his questions, not because he answered them, but because he spoke to Job and humbled him. Knowing God does not always make sense to our rational minds. Knowing God did not make Job's life better; for a while it got much worse.

5   *Thinking in the University*

The Lost Art of Learning

Peter Kreeft, Ph.D., is professor of philosophy at Boston College. In Kreeft's witty and insightful book *The Best Things in Life*, a twentieth-century Socrates visits a postmodern college campus and encounters a harried college student named Peter Pragma. Now Peter knows all the practical reasons why he's going to college: to get a good job so he can make money and have all the things money will buy, including a college education for his own children some day, so that they can get a good job and make money and send their children to college, etcetera, etcetera. But Peter Pragma is unable to see the futility of his circular reasoning, something that Socrates is trying to point out to him.

Peter: All right, wise man, or wise guy, whichever you are. You tell me. Why should I be here? What's the value of college? You've got a sermon up your sleeve, haven't you?

Socrates: Is that what you expect me to do?

Peter: Sure. Didn't you just tear down my answers so that you could sell me yours?

Socrates: Indeed not. I am not a wise man, only a philosopher, a lover and pursuer of wisdom, that divine but elusive goal.

Peter: What do you want with me then?

Socrates: To spread the infection of philosophizing.

Peter: So you're not going to teach me the answers?

Socrates: No. I think the most valuable lesson I could teach you is to become your own teacher. Isn't that one of the things you are here to learn? Isn't that one of the greatest values of a college education? Have none of your teachers taught you that? What has become of my great invention, anyway?

Peter: I guess I never looked at education that way.

Socrates: It's not too late to begin.

Peter: It is today, Socrates—or whoever you are. I'm really too busy today.

Socrates: Too busy to know why you're so busy? Too busy doing to know what you're doing?[13]

Peter Pragma typifies the average college student today, who is after an education for what it will provide by way of a job and a future. In fact, as Socrates pummels him with questions, Peter reveals by his answers—though he cannot admit it to himself—that everything he is pursuing is a means to an end. And yet there is no end that Peter can readily identify, other than some vague sense of happiness that the money he makes from the job he plans to land because of the studies he is presently working on will buy him. He is quite simply caught up in the means. One means to another means to another means. No one said it better than T.S. Eliot: "Where is the life we have lost in living?"[14]

Kreeft's Socrates is trying to interest Peter Pragma in a liberal arts education, without much success. When Peter wants to know why the liberal arts are so important, Socrates breaks from his normal pattern of asking questions and tells him outright that the liberal arts seek knowledge for its own sake.

Peter: That's... out of my ballpark. That "knowledge for its own sake" stuff may be a turn-on for you philosophers, but not for me.

Socrates: Are you quite sure? Look at your own standard again. How did you rank the sciences?

Peter: By how close to home they came. And liberal arts is out by the left-field foul pole.

Socrates: Let's see. Productive sciences improve what?

Peter: Things in the world.

Socrates: And practical sciences improve what?

Peter: My practice.

Socrates: And knowledge for the sake of knowledge improves what?

Peter: Nothing.

Socrates: Don't you see that it improves something closer to you than your practice?

Peter: No. What?

Socrates: What is the closest thing to yourself?

Peter: My underwear, I guess.

Socrates: Your self, is it not? Your *you*, your identity, your personality, your psyche, your soul, your consciousness, your mind. Do you have any idea what I'm referring to? You look puzzled.[15]

Peter Kreeft is pointing to a great loss in modern education—the loss of the art of learning. It begins long before college. In his discussion of current trends in American education on the Mars Hill Tapes, Charles Sykes, Senior Fellow at the Wisconsin Policy Research Institute and author of *Dumbing Down Our Kids,* pointed out that only 41 percent of a high school student's class day is spent on the actual study of academics. The rest has to do with what are called "basic life skills" such as handling money, self-esteem, and relationships—things that used to be taught in the home. He blames this "drift away from learning" on a major cultural shift that has turned America into a therapeutic society that "endlessly multiplies syndromes and complexes and therefore also multiplies treatments and therapies and nostrums of all sorts." The great American ideal of the pursuit of happiness has turned into a happiness to be achieved by entitlement, and schools must assist in the process. No longer interested only in education, schools have become social and therapeutic institutions, adjusting values and assuming the roles of nutritionist, nanny, and substitute parent. "Schools are failing, not for want of funding or order or hardware, but because school administrators have little time for the ideals of language, reason and truth."[16]

Dorothy L. Sayers, British writer, Christian, and robust enemy of uninformed and slipshod thinking, lamented the loss of discriminating thought in education as early as 1948, in her pamphlet "The Lost Tools of Learning."

> Is not the great defect of our education today... that although we often succeed in teaching our pupils "subjects," we fail lamentably on the whole teaching them how to think? They learn everything, except the art of learning. It is as though we had taught a child, mechanically and by rule of thumb, to play "The Harmonious Blacksmith" on the piano, but had never taught him the scale or how to read music; so that, having memorized "The Harmonious Blacksmith," he still had not the faintest notion how to proceed from that to tackle "The Last Rose of Summer."[17]

Sayers concludes her essay, "For the sole true end of education is simply this: to teach men how to learn for themselves; and whatever instruction fails to do this is effort spent in vain."[18]

Obviously this lack of thinking for oneself is not only a Christian problem, but mirrors a wider cultural challenge. Students today don't want to think for themselves; they are in school for a very clear practical reason. In some ways students are the premier pragmatists of the day. They want to get a job and secure a future. College students are paying dearly for an education, going deeply in debt to do so. The institution has the tools and the information they need to reach their goal; their professors have the knowledge to help them get there. These young people don't wish to be confused with notions such as "Question authority," "Think for yourself," or "Knowledge for the sake of knowledge." They are not in college to learn *how* to think. They are there to learn *what* to think that will enable them to get good grades that will unlock doors in a highly competitive and frightening world. Today's students have no time for exploratory learning. They just want to get it all down in their notebooks so they can pass the test.

Garry Trudeau covered the current college scene a few years ago in his popular *Doonesbury* comic strip. One Sunday strip pictures a lecture hall where "Wisdom! Wisdom!" is coming from the podium and "Wisdom received. Wisdom received..." is going into the notes of the students. Suddenly a turtle-necked professor appears in the middle of a lecture. "Of course, in his deliberations on American capitalism," he says, arms folded to reveal patches on his sleeves, "Hamilton could not have foreseen the awesome private fortunes that would be amassed at the expense of the common good. Take the modern example of the inventor of the radar detector. In less than ten years, he made $175 million selling a device whose sole purpose is to help millions of people break the law. In other words..."

And here he is interrupted by a student in the second row. "Maybe the fuzzbuster's a form of libertarian civil disobedience, man. You know, like a blow for individual freedom."

At this, the professor's eyes widen. "I... I don't believe it," he says.

"Believe what, man?" says the student.

"A response! I finally got a thinking response from one of you! And I thought you were all stenographers! I have a student! A student lives! Who are you, lad? Where did you come from? Don't be frightened..."[19]

The kid sits looking around the room as if something's wrong with him. Something is. He's thinking. He actually asked an intelligent question.

When I graduated from Wheaton College in 1969, in a class of 413 graduates there were twenty-three philosophy degrees, just over 5 percent of the class. Peter Kreeft's Socrates would have been pleased that at least a room full of students had been struck with the "infection of philosophizing." I recently attended the 1996 graduating ceremonies for the University of Southern California where over 9,000 graduates received their degrees. Among all those graduates, Socrates could barely get a discussion going. There were only six philosophy degrees given out, and all of the recipients were going on to a career in law.

Degrees earned over the last twenty-five years verify a major shift in emphasis. In 1971, there were 114,729 business and management degrees given by America's colleges and universities, or 14 percent of the total. By 1992, that number had more than doubled to 256,603, or 23 percent of all graduates. In contrast, social science degrees, the popular major of the '60s which gave students a general feel of the liberal arts, fell from 19 percent in 1971 to a lowly 9 percent by 1985.[20] Today one is hard-pressed to find courses that encourage students to grapple with the development of thought. Philosophy departments are nonexistent in many colleges, beyond perhaps an introductory course at the undergraduate level. In some Christian colleges, courses that touch on integrating subjects with a Christian worldview come not from the academic ranks but from student development departments run by deans of student life. The popular majors now are business, economics, communications, math, and computer sciences—skills that will translate directly into the workplace. In other words, education has been pragmatically reduced to the actual information one needs to accomplish certain real goals in an economic society where the dollar is king.

"Their Morals Were Never Engaged."

For his fascinating book *The Great Divide*, Studs Terkel interviewed a number of college professors in the late '80s. Aside from lamenting that their students got most of their information on Vietnam from Rambo movies and knew more about *Days of Our Lives* and *All My Children* than academic subjects, these professors seemed most appalled at the students' inability to take any position on an issue that might call for independent thinking. One of them gives the following account:

I brought up the My Lai massacre and (Lieutenant) Calley, who had been obedient to authority all his life. I gave them material on both sides, so they could make up their own minds. You could be shot for disobeying orders in combat. On the other hand, any reasonable man should know you don't kill hundreds of innocent, unarmed people. I tried to spark a debate: "How many of you think he should be found guilty?" A couple raised their hands, then a few more. Pretty soon all did. Guilty. I took the other side for a few minutes. "Now what do you think? How many of you think he's not guilty?" They all raised their hands. I got angry and argued the first side once more. I again persuaded them: guilty. I tried to engage them in debate. I changed their opinions four or five times. I was exasperated. They wanted to know what the teacher thought. I was the person in control and should know. I was the authority and should be obeyed. I was actually worried I was humiliating them too much. I never got through.[21]

That was not, by the way, at a Christian college. This sort of obedience to authority is not a spiritual virtue. It is a total abdication of personal preference, critical thinking, and opinion to the one in control. It is a deeply disturbing account of mental capitulation. The professor related two more examples:

> I tried another test on obedience and authority. I asked the nicest girl in class, the kindest, to step out of the room. I said to the others: "Your assignment is to write the nastiest things you can about her. You'll be graded on how scathing and insulting you are, how you can destroy her character. The people who pass this class are the ones who maintain a B or above. You also know the worst two will be read to her. Aloud. How many of you would go ahead and do it?" Just about all of them said they would. Without question. I asked them why. They said, "We want to get a good grade and we don't have to take this class again." Not one of them said, "Hey... you can't do this." Their morals were never engaged. Not one thought, "It would make the girl feel humiliated; my grade isn't worth that." It was simply, "Okay, this is authority telling me."

"Their morals were never engaged," he said, and that is not all. Their minds were never engaged. Their hearts, their wills, their reasoning processes, their consciences...

> I give people a chance to ask questions before the class ends. If there are none, they leave early. This ROTC girl was always asking questions—the rest of the class hated her. They would glance at her, look up at the ceiling, and roll their eyes: Oh... not her again. She was always challenging me. It wasn't that

they disagreed with her views. It wouldn't have mattered if it were a liberal student against a conservative teacher. They just wanted to go back to their dorms.[22]

It is a sad day for a generation when the heart to challenge has gone out of its youth. I wonder how different these scenes would be in a church or a Christian seminar led by an influential Christian leader. Something tells me it would be pretty much the same. Socrates would have a difficult time today because so few of us are thinking for ourselves. Our thoughts are not our own, but someone else's: a teacher's or a pastor's or a political leader's or a movie star's or a talk show host's. Everyone's thinking someone else's thoughts.

6   *Conclusion*

The "Redundant" Beatles

I was standing in the checkout line of the super-market when I heard a disturbing comment from a gentleman who looked to be in his late twenties. He was with his father (they were spitting images) near a special display featuring an anthology of Beatles music over the span of years in which they recorded. "I never really did understand the big deal about the Beatles," I overheard him saying. "They had a couple good songs, but most of their stuff was pretty redundant."

I just about dropped my cookies (and I wasn't buying any). Of all the words in the English language that could possibly describe the music of the Beatles and their contribution to American pop music, the word *redundant* would be the last. The Beatles originated almost every style of music that now holds a place in popular expression. In fact, whatever music the young man happens to like was undoubtedly influenced by the group he called "redundant." True, if all he ever heard was "I Want To Hold Your Hand" and "Love Me Do," you might say the group was redundant. But then you have to consider "Nowhere Man" and "A Hard Day's Night" and "Back in the U.S.S.R." and "Hey, Jude" and "Strawberry Fields Forever" and "Yesterday," covering every possible style of music from folk to hard rock to acid rock to ballad to string quartet. Oh, and while he was saying how redundant the Beatles were, a symphonic version of "Michelle" started playing over the supermarket speakers.

Now what if this man appears on a TV talk show and says in passing that the Beatles were redundant and everyone in their twenties and younger believes him? What if a generation that didn't grow up with the Beatles actually takes his word for it? Then the most powerful influence on a music culture in the last half century will be reduced to "a couple good songs, but most of their stuff is pretty redundant." When everyone thinks someone else's thoughts and no one checks it out, you never know what might end up being "true."

THREE

Whose World?

Since we cannot be universal and know
all that is to be known of everything, we
ought to know a little about everything.
For it is far better to know something about
everything than to know all about one thing.
BLAISE PASCAL

1 The Dumbing-Down of Society

As Dumb as the World

It is unfortunate that Christians are getting so much attention in a time in history when they are doing so little critical thinking. For the first time, probably since the Middle Ages, Christians are wielding power and influence in secular culture. Christianity is making itself known on the radio, in the newspaper, and on television as a powerful special interest group with cultural significance. It has moved into society through entertainment, into the media through politics, and into business as a strong consumer force. Contemporary Christian music is a highly marketable category, right up there with country music, jazz, black gospel, and rock and roll. A local nightclub in the Los Angeles area promotes one or two Christian shows a month into their regular weekend schedule, because they know they can fill the place with juice-drinking Christians.

Some see it as good news that Christians are gaining power in society. But the capsulizing of Christian positions by the press corps is not good for the Christian mind. It makes it harder to answer personally for our faith when there is a Christian voice doing it for us in politics, in education, in entertainment, and on TV. It's as if our beliefs are already spoken for in the marketplace. Ask the average non-Christian what a Christian is and what he believes and you are likely to get a longer answer than you would have twenty-five years ago, though it will most likely be an answer more identified with cultural/political issues than with things Jesus was known for like love, compassion, and healing.

The Reduction Principle

What happens when a group speaks for the individual? Complexity is simplified, issues are limited to a few emotionally compelling arguments, and consensus falls to the lowest common denominator. Of course, there is not a Christian political party in America, and yet a majority of born-again Christians today tend to be Republicans. Why is this? Is there something more spiritual about the Republican party? Or is it that the Republican party lines up better on the few common denominator issues that push the average Christian's hot button? What about other issues? If a politician is against abortion, does that mean he or she is automatically right about everything else? What if a politician is for prayer in school but against programs to help the poor, something that God made sure the nation of Israel took care of and one of Christ's major concerns?

If Christians were using their minds to make decisions about issues, seeking to make Christ the Lord of their political choices and responsibilities, wouldn't they be spread more evenly across the political landscape? Wouldn't it be a greater witness to the world if they were? To see that Christians can disagree politically and yet agree about the gospel would, in fact, draw more attention to the gospel than to a particular party's agenda. In *Prism* magazine Ron Sider writes, "People equally committed to Scripture disagree over specific legislation and social programs. This disagreement among Christians is legitimate and healthy."[1] I'm not so sure all Christians would agree with him.

There are those who believe that "one Lord, one faith, one baptism" should also be "one party, one agenda, one point of view." And even more disturbing is the attitude expressed in the press and even from the pulpit that party/agenda/point-of-view unity is more important than Lord/faith/baptism unity. For instance, in some Christian circles it's okay to disagree over the doctrine of free will, as long as you don't disagree with the current favorite political spokesperson. As Dwight Ozard points out in the same issue of *Prism*, "America is not crying for a greater plurality of Christian opinions in the public square; it is yearning for a Christian voice of integrity."[2]

But where will that voice come from, if no one is grappling with biblical faith and culture and politics? Where is the arena for the debate? Where is the forum to question or disagree? Does anyone want to? If we called for a discussion tomorrow about the Christian's responsibility to culture, would anyone come?

The problem is not only with Christians; it is within our society as a whole. The general "dumbing-down" is felt everywhere. The media speaks so loudly that no one else bothers to speak; and as the "experts" keep speaking, the average person is more and more pushed to the background and frustrated.

As the media tells it, politics is not about issues; it's about who's winning, who did what in the polls, who looked good on TV, who had the best sound bite, and what they thought of their chances. In an *Atlantic Monthly* article entitled, "Why Americans Hate the Media," James Fallows states, "The political sphere is nothing more than an arena in which ambitious politicians struggle for dominance, rather than a structure in which citizens can deal with worrisome collective problems."[3] Fallows writes about a CNN interview with a senator shortly after his announcement that he would not seek a fourth term. Since it was an election year, almost every question put to him by the news commentator had to do with the political implications of his departure and whether he was preparing for a run at the presidency. Each time he strongly denied any such intentions.

Midway through the interview [the senator] gave a long answer to the effect that everyone involved in politics had to get out of the rut of converting every subject or comment into a political "issue," used for partisan advantage. Let's stop talking, [he] said, about who will win what race and start responding to one another's ideas.

As soon as he finished, [CNN reporter Judy] Woodruff asked her next question: "Do you want to be President?" It was as if she had not heard a word he had been saying—or *couldn't* hear it, because the media's language of political analysis is utterly separate from the terms in which people describe real problems in their lives.[4]

There is a reduction principle at work here. The media will always pick the more compelling news item, and the political race itself will always be more compelling than the hard questions and ambiguities that face the winner once he or she is elected. Though the media is unparalleled as a disseminator of information, it also reduces everything that flows through its channels to the size of a TV screen and the length of a sound bite to compete with all the other sound bites. Os Guinness calls this the "CNN-ing" of society and it is one of the reasons Dick Cavett was replaced by Jerry Springer. This reduction principle seems to be at work everywhere.

Dumb and Getting Dumber

A rash of movies hitting the big screen in the early '90s celebrated a form of heroic stupidity. *Dumb and Dumber, Billy Madison,* and *Wayne's World* have all followed in the trail blazed by *Bill and Ted's Excellent Adventure,* which showcased the time travel of two high-school dropouts who had never heard of the major figures in history—exemplified in part by their pronunciation of Socrates as a two syllable word, "So-crates." Add to this string of successes the stupidly funny antics of Jim Carrey and you may have more than just a fad. Beyond making fun of stupidity, these movies turn the stupid person into a hero. Billy Madison is a twenty-year-old spoiled son of a billionaire who, having never gone to school, manages to graduate from the sixth grade in record time. The humor is mindless and unsophisticated. It takes little intelligence to appreciate these movies because they glorify a lack of intelligence. Is this humor an escape valve for a postmodern generation overdosed on information and dizzy with too many choices? Are these movies possibly unconscious parables of the lack of depth and insight that this information age is fostering? Or, are they a childish refusal to face into the seriousness of a society being torn apart?

Intelligent talk shows have given way to trash talk. Dick Cavett and Merv Griffin moved over for Phil Donahue, and now even Donahue is considered too intelligent for today's viewer. Jerry Springer, Geraldo, Sally Jessy Raphael, and a host of syndicated junkies and radio talk show hosts market emotional conflict for entertainment and profit. The more offensive, the better. A typical daytime talk show listing yields the following subjects: bad weddings, parents of dropouts, abusive husbands, meddling moms, romances, love troubles, hit men, multiple births, whining friends, family reunions, lazy kids, and viewers confronting guests. Civility and intelligent conversation has given way to mindless shouting matches of personal prejudice.

On March 9, 1995, Jonathan T. Schmitz went out and bought a shotgun, then blew away Scott Amedure, a man in his apartment complex who three days earlier had revealed himself as Jonathan's "secret admirer" on a live television show. Mr. Schmitz was angry because producers of the show had given him the impression that his admirer was a woman. He came out on stage before a studio audience and found a woman he knew. Figuring she was the one, he walked up and kissed her. But then he was told, "Oh, no, she's not your secret admirer. This is." And out walked Scott Amedure.

Patricia Auderheide, professor of communication at American University, commented on this tragedy. "What we have here is the retailing of emotional conflict for the casual pleasure of viewers. The consequence is human tragedy."[5]

Why this dramatic turn in our society? In an era when education and popular opinion have made a god of self-esteem, people are feeling more and more worthless. How can people watch others being trashed—even be entertained by it—and not be affected? We are witnessing a wholesale degradation of human life in the public arena and no one seems able to stop it. If there was ever a time for Christians to act intelligently as peacemakers, standing for respect and civility in a society where everybody seems infected with the virus of argument and the need for triumph, it is now.

2   *The Dumbing-Down of Christianity*

Christian Non-Think

And yet in the religious arena, a similar kind of dumbing-down is happening, with Christians often shouting as loudly and mindlessly as everyone else. The Christian Coalition commandeered the Republican state convention in Virginia in 1994, and among the slogans on the wall was this one WHERE IS LEE HARVEY OSWALD WHEN AMERICA REALLY NEEDS HIM?[6] Emotionally charged statements flood the Christian marketplace and end up on the bumpers, T-shirts, and hats of those who probably want to make a sincere statement of their faith, but are letting someone else do a poorer job of it than they could do themselves, if they used their minds.

A bumper sticker on a car in Denver reads, HOW CAN GOD BLESS AMERICA WHEN WE KICKED HIM OUT OF OUR SCHOOLS? Think about this. Who can kick God out of anything? If children can't pray out loud in schools, does that mean God no longer has access to the classroom? Is God licking his wounds and vowing he'll get even? "You think I'm gonna bless you after what you did to me?" Is this the God we find anywhere in the Scriptures? Seems more like Sylvester Stallone sulking in the corner of the ring with a black eye and a split lip.

But some will buy this bumper sticker for its emotional impact. They will hear the argument and never question what the statement implies about the deeper aspects of the nature of God. Now most likely no one is consciously demeaning the nature of God just to make a point on their bumper; someone is simply not thinking. Two people, actually: the one who thought up the slogan and the one who stuck it on the bumper.

But more than two people are involved. What about those who read the bumper sticker and like it? What happens to their idea of God? Without even noticing it, they have lowered their image of God. (God is out to get those guys.) And what about non-Christians who read the bumper sticker and *don't* like it, further convincing themselves that they want to have nothing to do with a God who worries about being kicked out of elementary school? What appears to be a harmless, catchy slogan can do a great disservice to the truth.

Another example of an emotional appeal with faulty thinking behind it comes from a Christian book on parenting I read recently, in which the author claims that he never argues about rock and roll; instead, he relies on God's Word. This position leaves no room for argument. If people want to debate the issue, he suggests they take it up with God. That's a pretty convincing argument, if it is indeed possible to know God's opinion on rock and roll. Personally, I would like to know God's opinion on many cultural issues like shopping, the arts, entertainment, and sports, items that have always presented problems for Christians who want a clear answer from God on every subject. Unfortunately, God didn't say anything definitive about football, movies, television, Mickey Mouse, pizza, roller skating, fat, the ozone layer, Democrats, rock music, and a myriad of other subjects.

But, like the bumper sticker slogan, the possibility of a clear word from God on rock music has an immediate emotional impact. It sounds good and it hits with power, as if someone finally put this difficult and delicate issue to rest. What Christian wouldn't respond to the final authority of the Word of God? The implication is that to disagree with this statement is to disagree with God. But a thinking Christian needs to realize that as tempting as it is to dispose of the problem so easily, God's opinion on cultural issues is never that clear.

Rock and roll as a form of music was invented some nineteen hundred years after the last book in the Bible was completed. Since there is no definitive passage on rock music in the Bible, we must fall back on related biblical passages, opening the door for interpretation and debate—a debate which should not be a threat to the interpretation of Scripture, but rather an important part of arriving at one's own personal belief.

Francis Schaeffer wisely said that where the Bible is clear, we must be clear; but on issues that the Bible is silent, we must leave the door open for discussion and individual leading by the Holy Spirit. To do anything more is to toy with legalism. That means we each have to do our own thinking and come to our own conclusions. The chances are quite good that we might end up in an argument with someone who comes to a different conclusion.

Actually, Christians could stand to have more civilized arguments on such matters. A better word would be *debate*. Debating one's position and listening to another's is one of the most important ways we formulate our ideas. My best memories of life at a Christian college were late night bull sessions with students from other denominations and geographical areas, as we engaged in the lively art of give and take. Having to constantly debate my position made me sharpen my critical thinking; almost always there was some stretching and compromising that brought every participant to a deeper understanding of the issues and of God's Word.

"For we know in part," says Paul (1 Cor 13:9), and this is why we disagree. Nobody knows completely. We all see only part of the truth, and to the extent that we do, we are partially right. When I close my mind to what someone else sees, especially a brother or sister in Christ who has the same Holy Spirit, I cease to grow in my understanding. I am impoverished when I hold onto my portion of truth, however true it might be, and refuse to listen to someone else's point of view. I am like the man who buries his talent and never finds out what is to be gained by investing it.

Argument is uncomfortable for those who feel there should be a clear Christian position on everything, and bothersome for those who do not want to do any of this work for themselves. We long for more definitive answers on these issues than we will probably ever get from God. In every discussion I have on Christian college campuses today about a believer's involvement in popular culture, I can almost set my watch by the arrival of the question, "But where do you draw the line?" To which I can only respond, "We should try to avoid drawing lines where the Word of God has not drawn them, nor fail to draw them where it has."

The author of the parenting book attempted to draw a biblical line on rock music where there is none. I can remember a twinge of uncertainty when I first encountered his statement, but I passed on it because the argument sounded so convincing. Who could object to standing on the Word of God? It wasn't until I listened to that twinge and went back to check it out that I saw something problematic in the argument. Now, I didn't have some great revelation from God. I was *thinking* about what I was reading rather then merely *accepting* it because it sounded right.

One has to wonder how often we respond to sermons without thinking. How many heads nod in automatic approval to weak arguments that would be uncovered by a few minutes of careful consideration? Sometimes the statements that sound the strongest need to be put through the most critical examination. Emotional statements often mask weak arguments. I am reminded of the pastor's sermon notes into which he had entered promptings: "Weak point, shout here!" No Christian should automatically believe everything preached in a sermon or written down in a book.

---

3   *Getting Smart*

More Noble

We read in the book of Acts that Paul rejoiced to find discerning believers in the Macedonian town of Berea. Luke describes them as being "of more noble character than the Thessalonians, for they received the message with great eagerness and examined the Scriptures every day to see if what Paul said was true" (Acts 17:11). They and the Scriptures became checkpoints for Paul's words.

Paul and Silas had just escaped a mob scene in Thessalonica where a few Jews and God-fearing Greeks "and not a few prominent women" had been persuaded to become believers; but the majority of the Jews were jealous over Paul and rounded up some bad characters from the marketplace to drive them out of town. Their jealousy predisposed them not to examine what Paul was presenting.

Many today are also predisposed not to think about what is presented in church, but for a different reason. The Jews didn't examine what Paul said because they had already decided he was wrong. Some believers today never hear their pastor because they've already decided he's right. The pastor is always right. His rhetoric is convincing. The seats are full. Everyone is buying it.

The Bereans examined what Paul said. They checked out his teachings with the Scriptures, and for this they were called noble in character—more noble than those in Thessalonica.

This nobility of critical examination recalls a verse in Proverbs where those who seek out the things of God are like kings on a quest, involved in a noble task. "It is the glory of God to conceal a matter; to search out a matter is the glory of kings" (25:2). God apparently puts his truth where it is not easy to find and then places a high priority on those who are desirous of going after it.

In Deuteronomy 29:29 we find, "The secret things belong to the Lord our God, but the things revealed belong to us and to our children forever, that we may follow all the words of this law." The truths God reveals to us are our privilege and our possession. The secret things have been entrusted to us and we are stewards of them (see 1 Cor 4:1). This is a high privilege and responsibility.

Knowing What Can't Be Known

Where did evil come from? If God didn't create it, who did? In the words of the Book of Ecclesiastes, why is so much of life so futile? Why does cancer strike one person and leave another alone? How could God make a human being for destruction? Such questions can make us shy away from thinking critically about our faith. Sooner or later we run up against one of these "unanswerables" and throw up our hands in desperation. The enigmatic nature of God's great wisdom alongside our finiteness often leaves us wanting to walk away from him and from these ambiguities. We don't have enough information, we haven't lived long enough, and some matters are simply outside our realm of understanding. Does that mean we give up trying to find out?

The human mind has a tendency to want to reject what it cannot understand. This is something Christians must learn to overcome for the simple reason that much of truth is paradox, or that which cannot be resolved in the human mind. Accepting paradox leads us to worship, when we realize our finitude and affirm God's incomprehensible wisdom. As Pascal wrote:

> If there were no obscurity, man would not be sensible of his corruption; if there were no light, man would not hope for a remedy. Thus, it is not only fair, but advantageous to us, that God be partly hidden and partly revealed; since it is equally dangerous to man to know God without knowing his own wretchedness, and to know his own wretchedness without knowing God.[7]

Pascal loved paradox and often spoke of it with fondness. We need to develop this same fondness for holding equivocal beliefs. Paradox is frustrating to us; some truths that coexist in the Bible cannot coexist in our minds. The free will and predestination controversy is probably the most famous. For every "Whosoever will may come" in the Bible, there is a corresponding "I have chosen you before the foundation of the world." "Work out your salvation with fear and trembling for it is God who is at work in you..." is another. How can two workings work together when one (ours) is not always conscious of the other? Then we think of the long string of biblical losers who win, the weak who are strong, the last who will be first, the blind who see and the seeing who are really blind, the poor who are rich and the rich who are poor, and the end which is actually the beginning. I believe that those who can embrace a paradox have the most fun with truth. It's only when we free our minds of having to resolve everything that we can begin to enjoy something of the mystery and grandeur and even the humor of the gospel. No one captures this paradoxical joy better than Frederick Buechner, when he compares fairy tales with the truth of the gospel.

In the world of the fairy tale, the wicked sisters are dressed as if for a Palm Beach wedding, and in the world of the Gospel it is the killjoys, the phonies, the nitpickers, the holier-than-thous, the loveless and cheerless and irrelevant who more often than not wear the fancy clothes and go riding around in sleek little European jobs marked Pharisee, Corps Diplomatique, Legislature, Clergy. It is the ravening wolves who wear sheep's clothing. And the good ones, the potentially good anyway, the ones who stand a chance of being saved by God because they know they don't stand a chance of being saved by anybody else? They go around looking like the town whore, the village drunk, the crook from the IRS, because that is who they are. When Jesus is asked who is the greatest in the kingdom of Heaven, he reaches into the crowd and pulls out a child with a cheek full of bubble gum and eyes full of whatever a child's eyes are full of and says unless you can become like that, don't bother.[8]

If we can't accept paradox, we will not accept the surprise of truth. We need to return to the creativity of children who have no problem with incompatible objects in the same picture. Their imaginations fill the incongruities with whatever happens to be around. This is how kids come up with talking animals and tree branches for magic wands. In the same way, we need to fill up what we can't resolve with our amazement and worship of an incomprehensible God who can do "immeasurably more than all we ask or imagine" (Eph 3:20).

Because we have a hard time holding onto contradictions, we naturally want to resolve them, both paradoxes and ambiguities, and yet we rarely can. That leaves us with two choices—to shut our minds down and hide behind simplistic answers, leaving complicated issues to the experts, confident that someone, somewhere is figuring it out; or, to learn to live with both ambiguity and paradox, training our minds to hold contradictions simultaneously and to live with the holes created by so many unanswered questions. Joseph Sobran says that British journalist G.K. Chesterton always defined things "without reducing them to abstractions; they keep their mystery even when they're known."[9]

This does not mean that we desert our attempt to understand paradox. It just means that we can go only so far until we cry out with Paul, "Oh the depth of the riches of the wisdom and knowledge of God! How unsearchable his judgments, and his paths beyond tracing out! Who has known the mind of the Lord? Or who has been his counselor?" (Rom 12:33-34).

There is a sense in which the more we know, the more we realize we don't know. In Pauline words this principle sounds like this, "The man who thinks he knows something does not yet know as he ought to know" (1 Cor 8:2).

I can remember back to a time when I knew more than I do now, not because I had more information but because I lived in a simpler world. I can still see myself as a young man and picture the swagger in my walk. And, I see it again in my teenage son. There is an arrogance in youth and in young Christians that can be described as untested faith—a faith that has all answers and no questions.

This is not to be confused with childlike faith. In an adult child-like faith is not naive. The old person who has such faith is still bent over by the weight of life's complexities. Faith does not obliterate these complexities, but it gives the stamina to believe in the midst of them. A simple faith is not simple because it has so few questions to answer; it is simple because it knows a God who can handle its many questions and the increasingly complex world in which it thrives. It's not what we know; it's who we know.

When I was a child, my family would take a long trip every summer from southern California to visit relatives and friends in Texas. We had a 1950 Ford, to which my father would attach a cylindrical cooler on the right front window to help us make it across the hot southwestern United States in August. He would also plan our trip to leave in the early evening so as to pass through the California desert in the cool of the night and arrive at our first stop in Arizona sometime the following morning.

My father drove the entire twelve hours himself... with my help, that is. By midnight the other three members of my family were fast asleep, but not me. These are, in fact, my earliest and fondest childhood memories—standing up on the front seat next to my father and having him all to myself. My eyelids were so wide open with wonder that they didn't even get heavy. You see, my father was a college professor, teaching mathematics and physics to big kids. That means when I asked him stuff about telephone poles and electricity and clouds and lightning and stars and planets and gravity and bug guts on the windows, he had answers. Did I go away from these sessions with fewer questions? No, always more. Was my universe more manageable because I got answers to my questions? No. It was less so, because usually the answers were harder to understand than the questions. But what I did get was a firm conviction of one thing: whatever question I had—whatever question existed in the whole spinning universe, for that matter—my father had the answer. Remove paradox and complexity and ambiguity and uncertainty from your worldview and you will miss the most important thing of all for a believer—moments like this with your heavenly Father.

Allowing for ambiguity and paradox in faith actually frees us to explore God's universe with an open mind. We don't have to resolve everything or connect all the dots. God's wisdom is not waiting to be proven by us; it does not need our ratification. Instead, it invites our discovery. It suggests that we come, see, explore.

There is more than one way to look at a thing. Jesus is the only way to the Father, but there are countless ways one comes to the knowledge of Jesus. We are always trying to homogenize faith, to make it fit our finite minds, and God is always pushing the envelope. He's not pushing the envelope of truth, mind you, but he's pushing us. Truth is always bigger than we figured on.

Ask, seek, knock, was the invitation from the Son of Man. Don't fear the unknown or the unresolved, for he is in control of it all. There is nothing too big for him, nothing that escapes his notice. He is, after all, the ultimate someone, somewhere, who knows everything about everything, and we are kings and queens on a noble quest to find out as much as we can about who he is and what he knows.

What's God Thinking?

When you love someone, you want to know what they're thinking. God is very important to me and I want to know him better. I want to be close to him. And, just as in any relationship, what he is interested in becomes interesting to me. Thus, as I fall in love with God, I fall in love with truth, knowledge, and everything I can wrap my mind around in the created universe, because this is his world.

My wife tells of how she came to know Christ through the library of a Christian man she was dating, even though he was taking a little vacation from the Lord at the time. She read his books because she presumed they were important to him. She says that had they all been about baseball, she would have read them just the same. Thankfully, his books were not taking the same vacation he was on, and my wife prayed and found Christ through the power and presence of the truth about God residing in this man's library. What he was interested in, or at least had been, became important to her.

So, what happens when I find that God is interested in the world around me? Naturally, I want to find out about that world. What happens when I discover he's been intricately involved behind the scenes of history all along? Suddenly history takes on new meaning. What happens when I realize that all scientific and mathematical knowledge reflects a world he created and an order he intended for the universe? That can only mean I have the potential of finding his smiling face hiding behind every equation and every problem that science presents. What happens when I see his image reflected in the fallen attempts at art and glory that come from people he has created? I want to identify that shattered image and seek to put the pieces back together so that I might know, and help others to know more intimately, what God had in mind for us from the beginning. What happens when I find out the lush rain forests he planted in South America with their intricately interwoven life forms are being systematically destroyed? I will want to do what I can to save them.[10] What happens when I learn that men and women he created are suffering the hunger and pain of war? I will want to know the truth about their situation and do what I can to help. As a Christian, as nearly and as often as possible, I want to look at the world and think God's thoughts. What he rejoices in becomes my joy. What breaks his heart breaks mine. I cannot love God and be detached from his world.

I find this challenging and exhilarating. We aren't required to know everything about everything. But if God is everywhere in his creation, as Scripture indicates and experience bears out, then knowing something about anything is a good beginning, and knowing something about everything is a commendable goal, even if it is always beyond our reach. Christians need to be Renaissance people.

4   *Conclusion*

Bring Back the "Renaissance Man"

The Renaissance of the eighteenth century in Europe produced major contributions in the arts, sciences, and philosophy. Learned minds dabbled in all the disciplines. The world of ideas and thought was waiting to be explored by anyone with the desire to know. Though the new belief in the importance of man carried with it the seeds of humanism, there were reformers in the church whose Renaissance thinking put God at the center of all truth. They saw both nature and grace as realms of divine activity.

The reformers called the natural sciences "the second book of God," and looked to it for the "hows" as they looked to Scripture for the "whys."[11] Most of the liberal arts colleges founded in the American colonies were Christian in orientation. Their purpose was to delve into God's universe and examine his ways. As in the earlier centuries of the Renaissance, much of the expansion of knowledge was accompanied by a sacred sense of exploring God's world. Today, we still call someone who dabbles in all subjects a Renaissance Man.

If, as Arthur Holmes of Wheaton College taught me, "All truth is God's truth," then God's truth is waiting to be found and identified by the searching believer. Truth does not come with a Christian label on it; it is truth because it is a part of the Father's world. The following words of Isaac Watts provide a fitting introduction to this world in which God is intimately involved. It is not a world of which he only occupies a portion. It is his world and he is everywhere in it.

> There's not a plant or flow'r below,
> But makes Thy glories known;
> And clouds arise, and tempests blow,
> By order from Thy throne;
> While all that borrows life from Thee
> Is ever in Thy care,
> And everywhere that man can be,
> Thou, God, art present there.[12]

God is present everywhere in his world. He is waiting to be searched out and found. Christians are people with an insatiable inquisitiveness who are interested in everything, because God is present everywhere that we are.

FOUR

One World

There is not one square inch of the entire
creation about which Jesus Christ does not
cry out, "This is mine! This belongs to me!"[1]

ABRAHAM KUYPER

1   *The Sacred and the Profane*

What You Pay Attention To

Mark Fenske is an advertising genius responsible for the images that sell the likes of Nike shoes, Wolfgang Puck pizza, and Aspen tourism. He feels that advertising is the most powerful art form in the world. A picture of Fenske in a popular magazine shows him holding up a hand-scrawled sign which hides half his face. The sign reads: "YOUR GOD IS WHATEVER YOU PAY ATTENTIO:".[2] The whole message doesn't fit on the sign. Getting the message across anyway, and seeing the irony of not paying attention to the available space on the sign, is exactly the art of it for Mr. Fenske.

He's right. Your God is whatever you pay attention to, and that is precisely the problem for the Christian who has to live in a demanding world and pay attention to a job, to finances, to family, to buying and replacing possessions, to the future, to retirement, and to insurance against calamity. It's a wonder anyone has any time left for God.

Perhaps there was a time when men and women paid attention to God *while* they lived and worked in the world. God was more readily seen in the fields and the valleys that he made, and in the sun and rain that determined the success of the crops. It's easier to worship him with hands in the earth than with hands in the guts of a copy machine trying to free a clogged paper feeder. To one who works first-hand with the things that God alone has made, the ties between work and worship are more obvious. But it's difficult to see God as having anything to do with global economy, power lunches, photocopiers, office politics, or Monday Night Football.

But do we find it hard to see God in the secular world because he's nowhere to be seen, or because we're not paying attention to finding him there? Just because we don't pay attention to him in all the aspects of our lives doesn't mean that he is not present. This is akin to thinking that we kicked God out of the classroom when prayer was banned in schools. When Christians leave God out of the secular arena of life, they probably don't want him there. It is rather like the '70s bumper sticker that read, IF YOU FEEL FAR AWAY FROM GOD, GUESS WHO MOVED? It's much easier not having to commit our secular activities to God's scrutiny, especially if we see them as being in conflict with him. In truth, God has not been left out of anything but our own thinking.

"There is no longer a Christian mind," says Blamires, and the first question has to be: Do we want one? When Jesus found a man crippled by the pool of Bethesda for thirty-eight years, he asked him if he wanted to be healed (see Jn 5:1-9). The question was valid, because the man responded with a string of excuses as to why he was still crippled after spending most of his life by a healing pool. A Christian mind, like a healing, comes with responsibilities that render useless our excuses for not thinking. A Christian mind might be too costly to our time, our efforts, and our commitments. Do we really want God encroaching on our work and entertainment? Are we willing to shed the excuses of a secular/sacred dichotomy that allow us to lay blame on a secular society? Do we really desire a new way of looking at life that acknowledges God in everything? Are we ready to be healed and walk out into the world and find him?

What if God is interested in the secular aspects of our lives as much as in the spiritual? What if he is as interested in what the swimsuit model did *after* her devotions as much as in the devotions themselves? What if going to work is just as important to him as our quiet time? What if he isn't a pop-up figure that folds back into our Bibles when we close them, but is truly God who sees all and knows all and is eager to share in our lives at every turn? If we believe God cares about our experience of human sexuality as much as we do, might we have a better idea what to do with swimsuits and pictures of women who wear them?

Where God lived a human life, he appeared to be anything but bored. I am sure the Son of God found meaning in every human activity, or else he would not have preferred the name "Son of Man." How could anything have been "secular" to Jesus Christ? Yet, was every activity he engaged in what we would call "sacred"? Did Scripture come out of his mouth every time he opened it? Was there a constant glow on the top of his head? Did heavenly choirs sing when he looked up?

"Your God is whatever you pay attention to" is only the human side of the story. God does not cease to be God when we're not paying attention to him. In truth, he is paying very close attention to us all the time. By returning the favor, we might just open up a whole new way of seeing things. We might just find out that it is possible to pay attention to God and the world at the same time.

Plato's Lie

Ironically, the major hindrance to seeing God in the world is a way of thinking that is almost universally accepted among Christians as a means to holiness. It is a dastardly trick because in pretending to provide us with a direct route to God, it hinders a real relationship with him more than any demon in Screwtape's camp.[3] I am speaking of the practice of dividing the world into sacred and secular compartments, so that "holiness" can be attained by a proliferation of sacred thoughts and duties and by a repudiation of the secular.

Many people do not realize that the sacred/secular dichotomy did not originate with Christianity. It had its beginnings in the teachings of Plato three centuries before Christ. The fact that the early church interpreted Christian teaching in the framework of Platonic thought is what has made people think Christianity was responsible. According to Ranald Macaulay and Jerram Barrs, "Every Christian meets it [Platonism] disguised in one form or another."[4]

When the early Christians read the New Testament, they already had a concept of reality made up of two parts—the material realm and the spiritual realm. According to Plato the material realm is a physical world that is imperfect, transitory, and shadowy. The spiritual realm is the realm of "ideas," or the perfect forms which stand behind the appearances of the material world.[5] The spiritual realm, therefore, is the reality behind the shadows of our material existence. The Gnostics pushed this to the extreme, totally discrediting the material world as being a complete illusion.

Thus early Christians could have easily interpreted New Testament warnings against worldliness, earthly passions, and the sins of the flesh as a denial of the physical realm, and they would have been tempted to push God into the realm of the spiritual. This was a mistaken interpretation—for them and for us. That sin is present in my body does not make my body evil. This same body can be given to God as an instrument of righteousness (see Rom 6:13) and it can house the Holy Spirit of God (see 1 Cor 6:19).

God created the world and called it good. He visited it numerous times and then actually took a human body and lived among us. Even in his resurrected form, he ate breakfast with his disciples and allowed them to touch his wounds. In fact, all of what God has done in human history, from Moses to the prophets to Christ to the eventual resurrection of our bodies, can be seen as a deliberate and calculated dismantling of the barriers between him and us that were erected as the result of our sin and disobedience. It was absolutely essential for our salvation that God embrace humanity in order to be a perfect sacrifice. In the process, by implication, he sanctified human experience. God obliterated the line between sacred and secular when the Word became flesh and dwelled among us (see Jn 1:14).

Satan, the archenemy of God's purposes on earth, knows that if he can reconstruct that barrier, even in our minds in the name of religion, he can keep God out of our lives and render us powerless. This is why John teaches in his first letter that the true test of whether a spirit is from God is its ability to acknowledge whether or not Jesus Christ has come *in the flesh*. Any spirit that cannot confirm this is not from God but is the spirit of the antichrist (see 1 Jn 4:2). Such a simple test renders the sacred/secular dichotomy as not merely inaccurate but demonic.

And yet we persist in believing that the material world is inferior to the spiritual one, that ordinary people who pursue earthly tasks are inferior to ministers and theologians, and that the way to holiness is to despise life, culture, nature, sex, and all material things. I believed all of this, and I am amazed to discover this thinking just as widespread among young people today. I am forced to conclude this false doctrine will continue to disguise itself among believers until the day Christ returns.

We have been created to enjoy God and his world in all its richness. To quote Barrs and Macaulay again, we have been created to glorify our creator in all that we do—

even washing floors. Everything we do as human beings is spiritually important. There is no sacred and secular. This does not mean merely that we see practical value in "secular" tasks like peeling potatoes and washing the floor. It means far more: God himself delights in them because he has created the realm of the physical. Therefore, we are to value every part of our lives just as he does. In fact, spirituality is to be expressed primarily in the ordinary everyday affairs and relationships of our lives.[6]

This is not just a way to get the most out of life. This is our purpose. We were made to glorify God in all of life. Any teaching or philosophy that leads us away from the affirmation of God's will in our physical existence is from a spirit that ultimately will deny that Jesus Christ came in the flesh. For if Christ came in the flesh, then we too can sanctify our human experience. To think otherwise is no less an error than to put ourselves in the company of demons.

---

2   *The Sacred and the Secular*

Combating the Sacred/Secular Dichotomy

In Titus 1:15 we read, "To the pure, all things are pure, but to those who are corrupted and do not believe, nothing is pure. In fact, both their minds and consciences are corrupted." Paul did not consider "sacred and secular" as inherent in the nature of things. If there is a line to be drawn between the two, it is in the mind of a person, the line that separates a pure mind from a corrupt one. A pure mind sees pure things, a corrupt mind sees evil, while both are looking at the same world. What is sacred or secular ultimately resides in the eye of the beholder and not in the nature of things or known by the labels we affix to them. What is sacred or secular is determined by the inner realities of the soul. The way our minds are oriented toward the truth determines what we see when we look at the world.

Lest you wonder if this one verse is adequate foundation to set aside one worldview for another, I would hasten to add that this concept is found often in the Scriptures. Proverbs says that the person who seeks for good finds good will, but evil comes to those who search for it (11:27). In other words, what you look for is what you get. In the Beatitudes Jesus said, "Blessed are the pure in heart, for they will see God" (Mt 5:8), a statement which echoes a psalm of David: "In righteousness I will see your face; when I awake, I will be satisfied with seeing your likeness" (Ps 17:15). Jesus is not talking only about seeing God someday in the future, but about seeing God now. Nor is he talking about some lucky sighting of God we stumble on from time to time, but a way of focusing on him in the midst of our everyday life in the world.

Think of Jesus, the Son of God, who walked this earth for thirty-three years among pagans and whores and lepers and evildoers, yet without sin. He did not require a pristine environment to protect him. He did not hide his eyes from the world. He had a sanctified vantage point from which to view the world and the people in it. Jesus could take in the world without having it alter his own inner purity. Otherwise, he could never have come here.

The see-no-evil, hear-no-evil, speak-no-evil monkeys in our common folklore come straight out of a sacred/secular model of reality. These fearful little guys must go through life deprived of their senses. They reveal a weakness not in society but in their inability to find what is good without being shielded from what is evil. They are helpless creatures who have no inner ability to discern for themselves what is right or wrong. They seem victims of an external world that preys upon them through their senses. If this is the path of purity, it is a most debilitating one.

In John 17, Jesus prays for all believers when he says, "My prayer is not that you take them out of the world but that you protect them from the evil one. They are not of the world even as I am not of it. Sanctify them by the truth; your word is truth" (vv. 15-17). As he prays for us not to leave the world, he also prays for us to be sanctified. It must then be possible to be in the world, surrounded by the world, and sanctified at the same time. This must have been how Jesus did it. Sanctification implies a separation, but it cannot be a physical separation, since he does not want to remove us from the world. If he had meant by this that we should be in some sort of protected environment where we would not have to be subjected to an evil world, he would have made that clear, and he also would not have had to pray for our protection. This is an internal sanctification he is talking about—a way of seeing. It is the same thing Paul was speaking of when he said that all things are pure to those who are pure on the inside.

Whatever Is True...

I remind you of the truth of the advertising man's sign: "YOUR GOD IS WHATEVER YOU PAY ATTENTIO:" If, in fact, God is not to be found in our "secular" world, then all Christians are subjected to idolatry for the better part of six days a week, and the seventh is going to have to be filled with a great deal of penitence in order to make up for the abomination of the other six. The only way to reach the holiness that God intends for us, short of taking all believers to heaven or tucking them away in a monastery, is for us to learn how to pay attention to God and the world around us at the same time.

"Whatever is true, whatever is noble, whatever is right, whatever is pure, whatever is lovely, whatever is admirable—if anything is excellent or praiseworthy—think about such things" (Phil 4:8). Those who quote this verse most often apply it in concert with the sacred/secular model as a call to cultural abstinence. Don't think about the world, they say; think about high and lofty things instead. They point out how impossible it is to indulge in secular society and pay attention to these admonitions at the same time.

But what is to keep this verse from being quite the opposite—a way of sanctifying our culture through the eyes of faith? Could we not go to a movie and look for what is right and find it in the portrayal of a sacrificial friendship, or a politician who morally compromises and loses, or a couple that stays together when everyone else is splitting up? Could we not watch a track meet and find something admirable in the God-given abilities of the runners? Could we not listen to "secular" music and find in a love song a sheer appreciation of the loved one's beauty? Could we not go to work and put our minds on what is noble in the completion of a job well done to the glory of God? Could we not watch a play at the theater and find what is excellent in the portrayal of the great human dilemma of good and evil? Could we not look for something praiseworthy in the natural talents and abilities of every human being we encounter? Could we not find all of these things while going about an average day in the world? Even while attending something as secular as a baseball game?

Extra Innings

The Ballpark in Arlington, Texas would not qualify as a place of worship for anyone but the most obsessed with the sport. And yet, as an average baseball fan who may attend no more than two or three games in a season, I was surprised to find a most plentiful array of true, noble, right, pure, lovely, and admirable things to think about at a recent game I attended there with a friend. And if these things were to be found in a ball game, how much more in the rest of our lives, if only we would learn to think this way?

Though I love the game of baseball, I don't attend many major league games primarily because I can rarely get anyone in my family to accompany me. I'm the only one with the patience to appreciate baseball. My rare chance for family company at a game is on my birthday or Father's Day when I request it as a gift and they have to go with me. The game I attended in Texas would have totally bored my family for seven and a half innings. All the runs were scored in the last half of the eighth and the top of the ninth innings. And yet that gave my friend and me seven innings to get reacquainted, since we hadn't seen each other in some time.

This is precisely why baseball is called America's pastime. It's a way to pass the time with flashes of interest bordering on excitement. This is one of the things that is *true* about baseball. It requires patience to play and enjoy. As in life, you have to weather the down times and learn to look for little nuances that give meaning to what some might find boring, such as the ball and strike count, the type of pitch thrown, the strategy of runners on the base paths, the decision of a manager to leave a pitcher in or take him out, the odds of a right-handed batter against a left-handed pitcher, the "brush away" pitch... and the list goes on.

Of all the popular sports in America, baseball is the most life-like. There is no clock, only twenty-seven outs for each team, and a game is never over until the last out has been safely tucked away in a fielder's mitt. That can take two hours or four, and technically, it could go on forever. And the season goes on for what seems like forever... a game a day. If you lose today, there's always another chance to turn it around. You think of that one time at bat that was squandered in May and cost a game. It didn't seem like much then, but in September when it comes down to one game's difference between a championship and a second place finish, and that game in May looms large. There are no unimportant outs. This is just as true about life.

Paul also wants us to think about what is *noble*, and there is still much that is noble about this grand sport. A few days prior to the Texas game, an opposing star player who is on a quest to beat the home-run records of Roger Maris and Babe Ruth wanted to keep a home-run ball he had hit into the stands for posterity. Normally when this is done, the player offers the fan who caught the ball another ball, usually autographed, in exchange. This particular guy had angered the Texan fans by taking the ball from the person and giving nothing back but a swear word.

The sports section of *USA Today* ran three articles about this incident, one of them telling how other players requested souvenir balls from fans. The most noble was Cal Ripkin, the "iron man" from the Baltimore Orioles, who has played more consecutive games than any other player in baseball history. On the night he set the record, he also hit a home run and requested the ball from a fan. In return he gave the fan a bat on which he inscribed, "Bryon, thank you very much for the ball. It means very much to me. We both share the same memory—homerun on 9-6-95. Cal"[7] A truly noble thing to do.

The night Ripkin was honored for his consecutive game accomplishment was a great one for what is still noble about baseball. He is loved by baseball fans everywhere for his commitment to one team during his entire career; his dependability to show up for 2,131 games without missing one; his commitment to family, community, and charity; his humble spirit, and his genuine love of the game. No wonder the play stopped that night for twenty-two minutes of nonstop appreciation. Everyone knew they were witnessing perhaps the last representative of a more noble era. Most young players today don't even know how to think the way Cal Ripkin thinks about baseball.

In baseball we encounter rules and regulations—right and wrong. Paul says to think about what is *right,* and in a society where what is right and wrong is left up to each individual's interpretation, it is refreshing to hear an impartial judge cry out, "STRIKE!," "BALL!," "SAFE!," "OUT!" without any regard to anything but the truth as it is spelled out in the manual of baseball. In the game we watched, the umpire made a dramatic third strike call against a Texas batter who let the pitch go by in a crucial situation with runners in scoring position and two outs. The umpire was flamboyant and loud, backing out of the batter's box, still in his low crouch, and thrusting his arms like pistons. "OU-OOO-T!" he shouted, and 35,000 people booed him, but to no avail. You could tell he relished the moment. That umpire was the only one in the right place to see that pitch and he called it, based on the rules and on years of experience. A call like this may be the last place in our society where we get a glimpse of Judgment Day when God will make the right call on every life.

Many people are also concerned about losing the purity of baseball. It's getting harder to remember the pure elements of the game, what with electronic scoreboards, artificial grass surfaces, luxury boxes, night games, and domed stadiums. If baseball lives on, it will be because fans remember the pure things—the smell and look of fresh-cut grass, the crack of the bat, the roar of the crowd, and the gravel-throated man in the stands behind home plate seriously questioning the umpire's ability to see anything past his own nose.

When we arrived at The Ballpark in Arlington, the sun was hitting the left field wall just above the scoreboard which follows other major league games inning by inning. This old-style board, with someone inside changing the numbers by hand is a purposeful return to a simpler era. Like other newer stadiums in Chicago, Denver, and Baltimore, The Ballpark in Arlington is trying to capture something of an older, purer day. As the sun glanced off the "Hit This Sign and Win a New Suit" sign at the 540-foot mark over the bleachers, a few gathering clouds were evident. As those clouds later gave way to the perfect full moon of a lovely evening, I realized that the admirable thing about this whole experience was that God had allowed for this enjoyment to be had under his sun, and I could give him praise for it and find worthwhile illustrations of commendable qualities to think about.

I Can't Get No...

I was doing my wife a favor by painting her office late one evening, with the radio tuned to a current music station to keep me company. I was not paying much attention to the music until a certain song came on the air that I had not heard before. I noticed it because the chorus was simply "Let's work," sung over and over to a driving, energetic beat. Due to the late hour and my flagging commitment, it was a timely message that put my work in a positive light. So I painted more vigorously accompanied by challenges to finish what I started, be responsible, and not give up. And as the song played on, I found myself thinking about the biblical concept of work—how Adam was cursed with work, how I could decide to see it as such, or choose to redeem it through the presence of Christ in my life. In effect, I preached myself a pretty good sermon on the value of work, even gave myself an "altar call" and "went forward" in my mind and committed myself to finishing the present task and arising earlier the next morning to accomplish my own. I can honestly say that the Holy Spirit ministered to me through the lyrics of this song and the ensuing discussion that went on in my head—all in the course of a three-minute pop song.

And then came the big surprise. The DJ announced that we had just heard a new release by Mick Jagger, lead singer for the Rolling Stones. Now such an encounter presents a difficult dilemma for the secular/sacred worldview which would deny that anything good was capable of coming out of the very wide mouth of Mick Jagger. A sacred/secular assessment of this moment would have forced me to conclude that I could not possibly have received any benefit from this song, since it was coming from one whose lifestyle and philosophy was antithetical to anything sacred. The song came from the same source as "I Can't Get No Satisfaction," "Honkey Tonk Women," and "Sympathy for the Devil." Even if Jagger had accidentally happened upon a song with some truth in it, the stamp of an evil kingdom would outweigh any benefits, and I was deluding myself to think that I could possibly be anywhere in the vicinity of God with that foul music playing. Who knows what deception victimized me while I painted? Like a monkey who is not supposed to hear any evil, I should have at least been tuned to a Christian radio station.

Or, is there another way to look at this? Did finding out the source strip away the value I had gleaned from this moment? Could I not acknowledge that regardless of what Mick Jagger had in mind when he wrote this song, I know what I had in mind when I heard it? I was able to confirm biblical truth about the value of work, and that was important to me.

This is simply one more time where the sacred/secular model proved inadequate. There is rarely a serious work of art, be it a song or a play, a film or a novel, that is either completely pure or totally depraved. Most of art—like most of life—ends up as a mixture of truth and error. One must learn to ferret out the good and the true while remaining on guard for the evil and the lie.

Christians who do this kind of critical analysis with art and culture train themselves to recognize these same warning signs in other areas of life. The writer of Hebrews has recommended such a discerning, practical approach to truth: "But solid food is for the mature, who by *constant use* have trained themselves to distinguish good from evil" (Heb 5:14, italics mine). "Constant use" does not mean constantly reading the Bible; it means constantly using the truths of the Bible to interpret the world around us. In so doing, we will discover both good and evil.

Popular songs can carry volumes of truth and even some practical advice, if we listen with a Christian mind. For instance, Don Henley's "Get Over It" can be translated as a refusal to give in to temptation or to get by a barrier to faith. Tom Petty's "I Won't Back Down" can be seen as an encouragement to stand firm in one's belief, as can R.E.M.'s "Stand." Neil Young's "Heart of Gold" is a reminder that no human being has perfect credibility. Indeed, even a song like "I Can't Get No Satisfaction" can be seen as a three-minute summary of the first three chapters of Ecclesiastes. What is the difference between Solomon writing, "I denied myself nothing my eyes desired; I refused my heart no pleasure.... Yet when I surveyed all that my hands had done... everything was meaningless, a chasing after wind" (Eccl 2:10-11) and the Rolling Stones singing "You Can't Always Get What You Want"?

Many of us have been trained to see God and culture in conflict—allegiance to one cancels loyalty to the other. No wonder so many Christians are frustrated and schizophrenic. We need to learn how to think about God while paying attention to the world. This is possible, but it will probably mean getting used to a much bigger God than the one many of us worship.

3   *Finding God in the World*

He's Got the Whole World in His Hands...

In chapter three we looked at the last verse of Isaac Watts' great hymn "I Sing the Mighty Power of God." Now it's time to look at it in its entirety:

> I sing the mighty power of God
> That made the mountains rise;
> That spread the flowing seas abroad,
> And built the lofty skies.
> I sing the wisdom that ordained
> The sun to rule the day;
> The moon shines full at His command
> And all the stars obey.
>
> I sing the goodness of the Lord
> That filled the earth with food;
> He formed the creatures with His word,
> And then pronounced them good.
> Lord, how Thy wonders are displayed,
> Where'er I turn my eye:
> If I survey the ground I tread,
> Or gaze upon the sky!
>
> There's not a plant or flower below,
> But makes Thy glories known;
> And clouds arise, and tempests blow,
> By order from Thy throne;
> While all that borrows life from Thee

Is ever in Thy care,
And everywhere that man can be,
Thou, God, art present there.

Isaac Watts' lyrics present a view of God as intimately involved with all of life. This God can be seen while looking down at the ground, just as when looking up. It is also a view of a world where a meal is as sacred as creation, where good can be found amid fallen creatures, where God's activity is evident everywhere, and where every living thing borrows its very breath from a God who is present.

Maybe it was easier to see the world and God this way two hundred years ago. In our postmodern, secular culture, the notion of God as intimately involved in the world is as outmoded as Watts' lyrics. But it's only we who have changed.

We are surrounded today by a world of our own making. Turn your eye in any direction and, unless you happen to be outdoors, most of what you see will be a product of human endeavor. But where did the ability to conceive and manufacture these things come from, if not from God? Where did the minds come from to create the technology that I rely on as I punch these words out on my laptop? Where did the minds come from that planned the manufacturing and marketing to bring this book into your hands? Did they not come from God? Are we not all, believers and unbelievers alike, still borrowing breath from the one who gives us all life?

My computer is an excellent case in point. Think about the people who have contributed to its existence. Imagine that not one of them is a believing Christian. In fact, some of them even now might be engaged in blaspheming the very God who gave them the ability to invent and perfect this piece of circuit wizardry. Does that mean that I cannot glorify God through the technology they made possible or acknowledge him for their ability to create it? They may not glorify him, but there is certainly no reason why I can't praise God for the resources their abilities have made available to me.

As a recording artist, I remember controversies in the early days of the Christian music industry over whether it was acceptable to use non-Christian musicians, engineers, and producers for Christian projects. Would a non-Christian guitar player cancel out or somehow dilute the message? Would the spiritual impact of a Christian singer be compromised by an unbelieving sound engineer? Would the Holy Spirit be blocked by a worldly producer? Would the devil leak into the recording through the fingers of a pagan guitar player?

Time has shown that Christians were not the only ones in line when talents were handed out. Some of the best players in the business, though not Christians themselves, have enhanced the music of Christians by contributing their God-given talents. And some have become Christians through their association with Christian artists and players.

Few ever knew it, but the major writer for a popular Christian singer in the '70s was an unbeliever. I know this because I spent many frustrating hours in discussion with him. This kind man loved being around Christians, though he would not become one himself. How could he capture the doctrines and feelings of believers without being one? Can God speak through the talents of those who do not believe in him? Hundreds of thousands of Christians who have been blessed by these songs over the years would have to say "Yes," even though their sacred/secular worldview might deny it.

Is God sovereign only when and where he is acknowledged as God? Or is he God regardless? Trying to explain God's activity in the world becomes increasingly ridiculous without an understanding of God as the giver of life and talent to all men and women as a form of common grace. One star running back does a haughty end zone dance after a touchdown; another bows and prays. They are both excellent runners, and their abilities came from the same God. The pride of the one does not have to ruin our enjoyment of his finesse as a runner. We know where he got his giftedness, and we can praise God for what the human body is capable of doing.

Looking for God in All the "Wrong" Places

We need to learn to see God in places where we have never looked before. If we do, we can turn all of life into a celebration of his presence. "Whatever is true, whatever is noble, whatever is right, whatever is pure, whatever is lovely, whatever is admirable—if anything is excellent or praiseworthy—think about such things" (Phil 4:8). *Consider these things as belonging to God wherever they turn up in the world.* In its simplest form, this outlook can be condensed into a phrase that I quoted earlier. "All truth is God's truth" was burned into my mind as a college student, and it has proven to be a trustworthy guide for integrating faith and culture.

Truth belongs to God wherever it is found. When we recognize anything in the world as being true, noble, right, pure, lovely, admirable, or worthy of praise, we can attribute it to God, and by that affirmation we can sanctify our experience of it. Our appreciation of life itself is holy as we discover God in it. When we can find something admirable in everything we do, we are finding God in our daily lives. Christians today do not need to spend more time away from the world to be holy. Instead, we need to train our minds to think about all of life in such a way as to *make it holy*. We do not need to do more spiritual things; we need to turn all that we are already doing into something spiritual. Brennan Manning has said, "Spirituality is not one compartment or sphere of life. Rather, it is a lifestyle: the process of life lived with the vision of faith."[8]

This vision of faith is a way of going about everything we do. The secular world is not a place to escape or evade; it is a place we are called to sanctify by our approach to it. The sanctifying of all of life is a more rewarding and engaging worldview than the sacred/secular model. The one takes place in a sheltered, safe, "sacred" environment where all the cultural decisions have already been made for us by the inventors and labelers of the Christian subculture. The other, a search for God which only we can perform, takes place from a highly vulnerable position in a very unsafe world. In one, the work is already done for us by someone else, perhaps in a book or seminar; in the other, we must do the work ourselves and depend on God to protect us.

Christians need to vehemently resist the passive approaches that are so common to our way of life. I often hear myself responding to the typical, "How are you?" with "Just getting by," or "Hanging in there," or "I'm surviving." Yet, finding God in our world is an activity that calls for mental awareness and emotional effort. Loving the Lord with all our heart, soul, mind, and strength does not mean just getting by. It means we are going at life with the intent of getting something of God out of it. If we are letting life happen to us, we are not finding God in it. Life does not "happen" to anyone. We either find God in it or we muddle through somehow. There is no middle ground.

Practicing the Presence

The joy in all this is that God will be found in the daily, mundane activities of our lives. If we seek him, we will find him; he has promised us this much (see Heb 11:6).

One of the most profound spiritual books ever written is *The Practice of the Presence of God* by Brother Lawrence, a cook and lay brother of the Carmelite Order. Those fortunate enough to have discovered this little treasure of a book over the last three hundred years have been treated to the inspirational example of one who consistently found God in the ordinary. Brother Lawrence's greatest insights were learned in the kitchen where he discovered the art of "practicing the presence of God in one single act that does not end." This metaphor of endlessness is understood by anyone familiar with housework! "I am doing now what I will do for all eternity," he writes. "I am blessing God, praising Him, adoring Him, and loving Him with all my heart."[9] If he could do all that while cooking and washing dishes in the kitchen, then we can certainly consider a similar focus, wherever we are in the world. Brother Lawrence believed it was necessary to talk with God throughout the day. There was no need to abandon conversation with God to deal with the world. His message still speaks to us today—whether we are flight attendants, teachers, writers, computer programmers, or students.

"The most effective way Brother Lawrence had for communicating with God was to simply do his ordinary work," observed his close friend, Joseph de Beaufort.

He did this obediently, out of pure love for God, purifying it as much as was humanly possible. He believed it was a serious mistake to think of our prayer time as being different from any other. Our actions should unite us with God when we are involved in our daily activities, just as our prayer unites us with Him in our quiet time.[10]

Brother Lawrence believed it is possible to pay attention to God and the world at the same time. This possibility is not merely a way to kill two birds with one stone, but it is essential, not only for spiritual growth but also for the mental health of the believer. Paying attention to God and the world at the same time is the only cure for spiritual schizophrenia, apart from leaving the world entirely. "Our sanctification," concludes Brother Lawrence, "does not depend as much on changing our activities as it does on doing them for God."[11]

Everything God Created Is Good

Another aid in this process of learning to see God in the world is found in one of Paul's letters to Timothy. In it he denounces certain teachers and their followers who abandon the faith by teaching demon-inspired doctrines about forbidding marriage and abstaining from certain foods "which God created to be received with thanksgiving by those who believe and know the truth. For everything God created is good, and nothing is to be rejected if it is received with thanksgiving, because it is consecrated by the word of God and prayer" (1 Tm 4:3-4).

In dealing with these false teachers, Paul provides believers with a means of affirming life. He argues that God gave us a material world to enjoy, and he directs his indignation at those who try to take that enjoyment away. This comes as a breath of fresh air to our current religious culture that tends to condemn the enjoyment of life's everyday pleasures. Indeed, I grew up around a Christianity that presupposed that if people were having fun, they must be doing something wrong. Here Paul puts the fun-busters in camp with demons, and affirms God's intention to give us good gifts to enjoy.

The simple statement *"everything God created is good"* offers glorious liberation, reminding us that God has placed a big "Yes!" on his creation. He affirmed it every day of creation, after making something new. And here Paul tells us it is still good. I have often heard the opposite message: that the world is bad. In one simple statement, Paul reaffirms what has always been true. In doing so, he announces that God's children can reclaim the original goodness of his creation. Paul follows his own admonition to look at the world and find what is true and right and noble and pure (see Philippians 4:8-9). You and I can also partake of God's good gifts and worship him with continual thankfulness.

There is only one true Creator, only one who can speak into the darkness and the void and cause a world to be, only one who can move upon the chaos and create order. He is the Lord God of Hosts. The rest of us can only mirror his creativity by arranging what he has already made in new and different ways. We create something out of something. We make charming quilts out of odd pieces of material. He creates something out of nothing. Though he pretends to be as powerful as God, the archenemy is merely one of God's creations like us. Though he wields considerably more power than you or I, this enemy is no match for God. He cannot create as God can; he can only twist. Satan has not created another world to vie with God's world, nor has he destroyed God's world. He took what God created as good and twisted it until it is slightly askew—until it gives glory to the created instead of the Creator. Our job, should we choose to accept it, is to take what the enemy has twisted and untwist it—to return it to its rightful position as that which gives glory to God. That is what Brother Lawrence did in his kitchen and that is where his joy came from.

This is what we can do with life, art, music, sports, food, fashion, gardening, the environment, and our many relationships. God wants us to sanctify the world, as we see it giving glory to him in all things. This is not only possible; it is essential. It is our mission in the world. How this mission works its way into our experience and our engagement in the world is the subject of the next chapters.

4   *Conclusion*

"Good Eye!"

Suffer me one last baseball illustration. When a batter lets a close pitch go by and the umpire calls it a ball, that noisy guy behind home plate—you know, the one who looks over the umpire's shoulder, making him the umpire's umpire—cries out, "Good eye!" It was a bad pitch and a good eye caught what was bad about it.

Good batters have inexhaustible patience. They've studied up on the pitcher. They have an idea what he likes to throw in certain situations and they can "read" the ball coming off his hand or the certain twist of his elbow that gives away a fastball or a curve. A split second of recognition can be a huge advantage. Good hitters aren't lucky. They're knowledgeable and patient.

The world is full of bad pitches, but Christians who have done their homework have learned how to develop a good eye. They know what they can use of what the world throws at them, and they know what to let go by. Jesus said, "The eye is the lamp of the body. If your eyes are good, your whole body will be full of light" (Mt 6:22-23).

Your God is whatever you pay attention to. Yes, we must pay attention to the world, but in doing so we pay attention to God, for in spite of its fallenness,

This is [still] my Father's world. He shines in all that's fair.
In the rustling grass I hear him pass; he speaks to me everywhere.[12]

FIVE

Finding the Unknown God

Christians should not fear the idols
and myths of our day, as long as they
have no reverence for them.[1]
KENNETH A. MYERS

1   *How the World Sees Us*

"The Christians Are Coming"

Bob Dylan could have had Christians in the '90s on his mind when he penned his famous putdown, wishing that for just once the offending party would stand inside the other's shoes and discover what a drag it is to see themselves from another vantage point. Indeed, it does appear as if Christians these days have nonbelievers on the run, and the secular press is behaving like a mad band of Paul Reveres, announcing at every turn, "The Christians are coming! The Christians are coming!"

For a long time, Christians in America stood by and watched the secularization of a society which we believe was once a God-fearing nation. And then, in the spirit of the movie *Network,* we decided we simply were not going to take it anymore. Though it's debatable whether the founding fathers had the same America in their minds as many do today, the important thing is that Christians feel our country is being taken away from us, and for the first time in decades, we are tasting the heady sensation of discovering we just might be able to do something about it.

World on the Run

A number of elements have come together in the last twenty years to boost the power of Christians in America. The growth of the Christian subculture has spawned a new network of centralized communication. Christian radio stations now crisscross the country, giving their version of the news and sensitizing believers from all persuasions and denominations to hot political issues. Pulpits and neighborhood marches encourage Christians to stand up and be counted in society. Popular radio and television teaching programs have access to millions of homes and automobiles, and Christians are now discovering that the media's power to mobilize can be effectively channeled toward Washington. What was begun by the Moral Majority is now being fine-tuned by the Christian Coalition—a group which gains strength from other powerful conservative forces in society.

For more on the causes and ramifications of this new socioreligious battlefield, you may want to consult *Beyond Culture Wars* by Michael S. Horton. For the purposes of our discussion, it is important to understand that the cultural climate in America today is one of societal combat. We live in an age of racial, political, religious, and ethnic culture wars, of angry rhetoric and hate-filled pontification. The battle lines that Buffalo Springfield sang about thirty years ago are being drawn again. Nobody's right in a society filled with wrong attitudes. Who knows but that the wars Jesus said would fill the last days are not full-scaled armed combat, but the dogmatic, one-sided, ideological skirmishes that are presently polarizing society on almost every level.

If we are going to represent the gospel to this culture, we need to realize that we start with a perception among non-Christians that is antithetical to our message. Non-Christians today think that many Christians are out to get them, not because they are lost and need to be found, not because they are lonely and need a friend, not because they are dying in their trespasses and sins and need to be saved, but because they are wrong and need to be either set straight or defeated. If we want to be sensitive to Christ and the gospel, we need to reexamine how we think about non-Christians.

2 *How We See the World*

The World Is Not Wrong As Much As It Is Lost

In a culture war of issues, it is easy to forget that the world is made up of men and women for whom Christ died. It was because of the sin and lostness of humanity that Jesus came to redeem us—to buy us back with his own blood. He came because God loved his own and did not want to see us die in our trespasses and sins, a death that was nevertheless required by his holiness and justice. And so the death of Christ in our place made a relationship between the Creator and his creation possible. It was all motivated by love—God's love—his desire to save that which was lost. This is the central message of the gospel.

A southern California evangelistic crusade was recently pegged by an editorial in *The Los Angeles Times* as a rally to gain support for the Christian right. Those who attended heard only the message of the gospel. But those who did not attend heard something else. Now when the eternal salvation of someone's soul is perceived as a means of garnering another vote, something has surely gone awry.

If we are concerned about getting the gospel out to the world, we will have to change our attitudes about the world. We need to see the world not so much as wrong as it is lost. More than anything else, this will influence the way we operate in the world. Christians must not participate in the attitudes of ideological and moral superiority that permeate our present society.

Yes, of course, the world is wrong, but then so are we. Nor is the world wrong about everything, just as we Christians are not right about everything. We need to get off the morality track and back onto the gospel track. Moral issues are important, but they are not the reason for the cross. Jesus did not die to create a more moral universe. He died to save us—so he would not have to destroy what he made in his own image. Our present culture is focused on political, ethnic, and religious rightness and wrongness. The gospel is all about being lost and found.

The way we think colors the way we act. If we believe someone is wrong, and we are on a personal mission on their behalf, our purpose will be to set them straight. Such a tactical mission requires no personal involvement, it is devoid of compassion, and carries with it a spirit of arrogance.

Often, our evangelistic attempts in the world are done from this perspective. If we are trying to set the world straight we won't see ourselves as living in the world, nor will we befriend non-Christians and dialogue with them in nonthreatening ways. We won't listen to and respect other people's beliefs and wait patiently for an opportunity to share ours. We will more likely remain in the safety of a Christian subculture and avoid relationships with non-Christians that we aren't actually forced to have.

And when we do go out with our message, it will look more like a raid than a compassionate search for those who are lost. If we believe that we are right and everyone else is wrong, we put the world on the defensive. This is not so much "Seek and save that which is lost" as it is "Search and destroy that which is wrong," and that which is threatening to our lifestyle as Christians.

Seek and Save

"Today salvation has come to this house," Jesus said to Zacchaeus, after he found the man up a tree and invited himself to his house, much to the chagrin of the people who knew what a sinner Zacchaeus was. "For the Son of Man came to seek and save what was lost" (Lk 19:9-10).

When you think of someone as lost, you have a different attitude toward her than if she is wrong. You don't try to set her straight; you try to find her and bring her safely home. Jesus had compassion on the multitudes because they were like sheep without a shepherd. He didn't put them in religious or political camps. They were not Romans or zealots or Gentiles or liberals or conservatives. They were lost. His favorite stories, the ones that seemed to capture the heart of God toward sinners, were of finding lost things. The shepherd who left ninety-nine sheep in the pen to look for the one that was still at large (see Lk 15:3-7); the woman who persisted in finding the missing coin (see Lk 15:8-10); the man who found a treasure in a field and got so excited he buried it again, sold everything he had, and bought the field (see Mt 13:44); the merchant who sold all his possessions to buy one pearl of great value (see Mt 13:45); and, of course, the most famous of all, the father who welcomed his wayward son home with nary a word of criticism or condition, only celebration over the homecoming of his son who was no longer lost (see Lk 15:11-24).

Looking for something that was lost implies that the object has value. Why would a woman work so hard just to find one coin? I find coins in the laundry all the time—sometimes even dollar bills. We call it laundered money in my family. When I'm out and about in the car, I can rummage around under or between the seats for at least fifty or sixty cents if I need it. Why spend so much time looking for one coin? This coin must have been important to her, must have had great value. Imagine the joy of discovering that you are that lost coin and that someone has been looking for you all your life and you didn't even know it! This is what happens when sinners find out that they have been very important to God for a long time.

We fail to communicate this importance when we only try to set someone straight. There is little personal involvement in proving someone wrong. There is only the smug satisfaction that we have once again made our point. But when we search for and find something lost and of great value to us, we are less inclined to lose it again. That which has been found becomes an integral part of our life. A lost relationship has been restored, never to be lost again.

The World Is Right About a Lot of Things

As we learn to listen more intently to our culture, we discover that people are closer to the gospel message than we may have realized. The world makes self-assessments that we can affirm, and when it comes to being lost, the world can often capture this better than we can.

Christians have always liked to write "before" and "after" conversion songs. Some of my earliest songs were of this type, dealing in part with what it's like being lost. And yet, for a Christian being lost is something of a memory. It's hardly necessary to try to remember what it was like to be lost when there are so many non-Christians expressing it already. They don't have to remember anything, merely report what it's like to be where they are. No one can paint a picture of being lost better than someone who is lost and cannot see the way. Like Blind Faith, who in the '70s sang, "I Can't Find My Way Home," each generation has had its lost artists crying out. Joni Mitchell in her song, "Woodstock," tried to find her way back to the Garden of Eden. Sting sent an S.O.S. to the world in his song "Message in a Bottle." And grunge and punk artists of the '90s carry a common theme of alienation.

In many ways, the world is its own best critic. The keenest indictments against the world come from the pages of its journalists, commentators, artists, and comics. The funny pages of a newspaper can convey the most scathing of social criticism, showing how the world's attempts to solve its own problems often come up short.

Take for instance the cartoon *Non Sequitur* by Wiley, which has a frumpy gentleman walking up to a rack of books titled "Self-Help Books" in a "Nineties Lifestyle Bookstore." On the shelves are titles such as: The Magic of Rudeness, Screw Everyone, Just Say No to Conscience, I'm OK—You're Not, How to Blame Society, The Joy of Narcissism, It's Only Wrong If You Get Caught, Everything Is Your Parents' Fault, and Sociopaths Are People Too! Even a Christian world overly enamored with pop psychology could stand a splash in the face from such poignant warnings. Or, how about the two gunslingers in an OP/ED page cartoon facing off next to a corral of horses where one fires off the first round: "You need to get in touch with the hurt child within yourself," and the other shoots back with, "I'm sensing a lot of hostility here..." The caption reads, "Trouble at the I'm OK, You're OK Corral." The world knows when its own idols prove false and doesn't need anyone to tell them. Just listen to Don Henley sing about wanting to kick the little behind of the next guy's inner child, and you can hear the world question its own therapists.

I carry around an *Outland* cartoon by Berkeley Breathed that shows, better than any evangelistic sermon I have ever heard, the difficulty human beings have paying attention to their ultimate destiny. In it Opus, the little penguin character with the beanie, is looking at a magazine ad with his friends and confesses, "I was just sittin' here wonderin' if there could possibly be anything more important in life than owning an overhead cam six liter Porsche 969 SX.... Then I thought of Michael Landon. Suddenly he had three months left. I'll bet he figured out quick what was really important and what wasn't. So why don't we figure it out when we have lots of time left?" One of his little companions says, "Yeah," and then for a silent frame, the three friends lie back on a hillside and stare up at the sky thinking about their eternal destiny. In the final frame, Opus raises his head and looks at the Porsche again and says, "Red." To which another replies, while still staring at the sky, "Gotta be red." In one brief cartoon, we are all forced to face the power materialism has to drown out the deeper questions.

Christians need only take Bob Dylan's advice and stand inside the world's shoes for a moment to see truth from another perspective. We can benefit from learning to do this, because when the world is being truthful, it sometimes catches us in hypocrisy or compromise. The unbeliever who stares up at the sky and faces the silence could be more in line with biblical truth than a believer distracted from spiritual things by chasing after a red Porsche.

Whose Shoes?

When the world faces its lostness head-on, the most honest answer is often despair; and down through history, artists have had the most courage in confronting this dark message. Christians often misjudge this fact when trying to evaluate culture.

For instance, some Christians think of a song like "Lean on Me" as being more in keeping with the gospel message than a dark, demented song by Trent Reznor, when, in fact, it can be argued the other way around. Facing the despair of life without God might bring an unbeliever closer to the gospel than leaning on a friend. As the last rung on the ladder, despair can bring a person to cry to God for help. When we fail to stand inside the shoes of the world, we sometimes condemn true expressions of desperation that could open unbelievers to the gospel. At the same time, we may approve of shallow expressions of wishfulness that postpone one's need for God. Despair may do a person more good than a false hope.

Christians will hear a song like "Lean on Me" and think of God, and rightfully so. But we should also realize that not everyone is thinking about God when they hear this song. Stand inside the world's shoes and listen to "Lean on Me" and you hear a good song about people needing each other to get along in life. A good concept and helpful to Christians and non-Christians alike. But if a song like this leads people to believe that with the help of others they can make it in life without God, then it is the most insidious message of all. Passengers holding onto each other in a burning plane may feel some comfort, but they are still going down.

3   *What the World Thinks*

Longing for God

Much of the art of thoughtful non-Christians expresses a longing for God. Any story that has to do with a moral universe where good struggles with evil, for instance, can be seen as a longing for God. But the world is often inconsistent about this. On the one hand scientific theory assumes an amoral universe while on our movie screens, from *Star Wars* to *Lion King,* good almost always wins out over evil. Science can't even come up with good and evil, much less make one of them win.

In Ecclesiastes, the Teacher pinpoints a common human frustration. "I have seen the burden God has laid on men. He has made everything beautiful in its time. He has also set eternity in the hearts of men; yet they cannot fathom what God has done from beginning to end" (3:10-11). When artists reach into their colors or to the notes of a musical score, into the developing solution in a darkroom tray or to the flow of words on a page, they are interacting with the eternity God has placed in their hearts. They are trying to be significant in the universe—trying to mean something more than a random collision of molecules. Though modern philosophy tells them they are nothing, their hearts tell them something else. Because their minds cannot fathom what their hearts know, they feel the weight of the God-placed burden. Art often seems irrational, because the heart is reaching beyond the mind. A modern art museum displays the heart reaching beyond what the mind knows, trying to find the meaning of its existence.

All of this is simply one more frustration that God has placed on his creation so that it might be forced into reaching for him and perhaps finding him, "though he is not far from each one of us" (Acts 17:27). It is why the Teacher of Ecclesiastes was thwarted at every turn, trying to answer the questions of his heart with his mind only. He kept coming to the same conclusion: "'Meaningless! Meaningless!' says the Teacher. 'Utterly meaningless! Everything is meaningless'" (1:2).

Such conclusions turn up everywhere in society and yet Christians often paradoxically condemn these messages. They accept similar conclusions from the Teacher of Ecclesiastes but fail to make the connection with our society. If the great King Solomon cried, "Meaningless!" thousands of years ago, we need not think that those who cry it today are so far from the grace of God. If we can understand these words as fitting into the scheme of biblical revelation, why can't we understand them in the context of our contemporary culture?

The most current music of today, the punk, grunge, and industrial metal music of a lost generation, proclaims a nihilistic message. This music would resonate with the dark cry of Solomonic despair about the meaninglessness of life. When we don't acknowledge that these same words are in our Bibles, we fail to see the Bible as a story of human beings seeking God and God seeking us. Why is Ecclesiastes in the Bible? One reason might be to show how one man went systematically through the basic questions of our existence and came, in the end, to the only reasonable thing to do: "Fear God and keep his commandments" (12:13). Those who have been found should not thwart the process of seeking and finding in others.

Christians need to be more patient with non-Christians since they may be in the process of coming to know God. Paul said there are only two kinds of people: those who are being saved and those who are perishing (see 2 Cor 2:15). That means that a lot of non-Christians are in the process of being saved, and we (and they) don't know it yet. We need to patiently wait for this process, while we watch for the "reachings" of those who may be seeking God but are unwilling or unable to identify their search in our terms.

To an Unknown God

We need a vision of God big enough to connect him to the false gods and the secular poets of our day, as Paul did. While Paul was waiting for Silas and Timothy to join him in Athens, he reasoned with the Jews and God-fearing Greeks in the synagogue as well as with people in the marketplace. He had been observing their culture and was "greatly distressed to see that the city was full of idols" (Acts 17:16).

A group of Epicurean and Stoic philosophers heard of his strange ideas and decided to invite Paul to a meeting of the Areopagus, where "all the Athenians and the foreigners who lived there spent their time doing nothing but talking about and listening to the latest ideas" (v. 21), what you might call an ancient precursor of the television talk show.

Given how upset Paul was over what he found in their city, his opening lines take us by surprise. "Men of Athens! I see that in every way you are very religious. For as I walked around and looked carefully at your objects of worship, I even found an altar with this inscription: TO AN UNKNOWN GOD. Now what you worship as something unknown I am going to proclaim to you" (vv. 22-23).

Paul did not reproach them for their idolatry, even though

he was "greatly distressed" over it. For reasons of the gospel, he kept his indignation to himself. Contrast this attitude with that of Jonah who, when God sent him to save a similarly wicked generation, got upset that they actually repented. Jonah wanted to be the prophet of doom and gloom and bring the fire of judgment down from heaven on their wickedness. When God decided to save the people, Jonah went off and sulked.

Paul wanted the Athenians to know about Christ. When faced with their culture, and a myriad of sins he could have rightfully charged them with, he chose instead to start with the one thing he could affirm that would open up a way for the message of the gospel.

There are so many things wrong with our culture today—so many things Christians could be distressed about; and yet, in light of every person's eternity and what Jesus has done for us all on the cross, these evils are not what we should be focusing on. Since Christ has already died for all of the sins the world could ever come up with, the issue is to let people know they do not have to pay for their sins themselves.

Some Christians today appear to be contradicting this attitude by gloating over the rise in AIDS among the homosexual community, as if these people are getting their just reward. What should be on the heart of every Christian is a compulsion to let dying people know that they don't have to pay what is due on their sins, since Jesus already paid it. This is the message of the gospel and what motivated Paul to look past the idols of Athens. Michael Horton has said it well, "I have always wondered why any homosexual would listen to us when we talk about AIDS as the judgment of God, musing at what a lucky thing it is for the rest of us that God does not hand out diseases for gossip, greed, or self-righteousness."[2]

A good attitude test for Christians today is to ask: What if God decided to suddenly save all the abortionists, gays and lesbians, militant feminists, and atheists who want to eradicate all signs of Christianity from public life? What if they suddenly showed up in church on Sunday with a soft heart toward God and a receptive ear to the gospel? Would we be overjoyed? Would we welcome them with open arms or would we go off and sulk? Jonah's problem was that he found his identity in being at odds with Nineveh; when God changed the heart of the city, Jonah was out of a job. I sometimes wonder if the church is opting for the same negative job description today.

Very Religious?

It wasn't much, but Paul found something positive to say about the sorcerers and idolaters and secular philosophers of Athens: "I see that in every way you are very religious" (Acts 17:22). Could it not be said of our generation as well? Aren't people looking for spiritual answers right now? They may be looking in the wrong places, but aren't they open to the supernatural? A person on a spiritual search may not be talking about anything more than a desire for meaning that acknowledges the nonmaterial dimension; and yet, such a search can be thought of as positive. Are there areas in which we could turn to our society and say, "I see that in every way you are _____," (perhaps "concerned about the poor," or "very value oriented," or "looking for spiritual answers," or "disappointed in some of the supposed answers of popular psychology")? These are places where a discussion can begin in the Areopaguses of our world.

Steve Turner, in his book *Hungry for Heaven: Rock 'n' Roll and the Search for Redemption,* takes a spiritual approach to the history of rock 'n' roll from the '60s to the present. He shows how a hunger for spiritual truth has been at the core of rock music since its beginnings in the Pentecostal churches of the South. In his introduction, Turner suggests a link between St. Augustine's statement, "Man was made for God, and his heart is forever restless until it finds its rest in him" and Bruce Springsteen's song, "Everybody's got a hungry heart." In his final chapter, Turner points out, "Few would doubt that the 1990s are witnessing a renewal of interest in religious experience, from books on encounters with angels to the mysticism of the new physics."[3] This interest may not be the hungering and thirsting after righteousness that Jesus spoke of; however, it acknowledges an inner need and desire to look beyond this fallen world for meaning. It offers us a way of saying to our present culture, "I see that in every way you are very religious." If Paul could recognize in an idol a hungering for the true God, then rock music might be a place where we could look for an unknown God in our current civilization.

Robert Capon thinks that the world is anxious to believe; they are simply not interested in hearing about the moral issues which seem to be the church's current theme in the world.

> The modern world is dying to believe. People surreptitiously read People magazine in the checkout line precisely because they are itching to believe the most unbelievable stuff as long as it's astonishing. They will believe in reincarnation, transmigration of souls, New Age spiritualities, and regression to past lives because they find those oddities more interesting than the predictable faith-and-morals pap we persist in handing them instead of the paradoxes of the Gospel.[4]

The idea of an "unknown" God is a curious one, especially in a pagan culture. It suggests that people recognize the existence of God—perhaps even their need for God—without any knowledge of who he is or how to find him. Like Athens, America is a pagan culture; but unlike Athens, we have a Judeo-Christian memory. Sometimes the world is looking for God but has a hangup with its memory which tends to confuse God himself with many bad examples of Christians or unfortunate experiences in church. We need to listen carefully to our culture, as Steve Turner has done with rock music, to see if what the world is calling by another name might, in fact, be a hunger for the God we know in the Scriptures.

A Starting Point

As we look for what we can affirm in our culture, we have much to choose from. The memory of faith from earlier generations keeps leaking through. The present Christian force in politics, for instance, is empowered in many ways by the memory of a time when Christianity played an important role in society. Though a Christian moral influence should never overshadow the gospel (morality never saved anyone), the desire for a moral universe prevails in our society. Christians can begin the discussion here.

People who are not Christians care about others who are less fortunate. Christians and non-Christians share a common compassion for the victims of war, violence, and abuse. The gospel is saturated with similar concerns. Jesus announced his mission on earth by stating that the Spirit of God had anointed him to "preach good news to the poor... to proclaim freedom for the prisoners and recovery of sight for the blind, to release the oppressed, to proclaim the year of the Lord's favor" (Lk 4:18-19).

Christians entering into discussion about the environment can point to their personal relationship with the Creator God as a primary motivation for their interest in safeguarding the world God has made. Sports and recreation sometimes border on obsession in our culture, and yet Christians can glorify God in their bodies and run to his glory, as Eric Liddell did. His story was compelling enough that it won an Oscar as the movie *Chariots of Fire.*

If we listen carefully to our culture, we can find many places to enter the discussion and turn it toward Christ, just as Paul did in Athens. "For as I walked around and looked carefully at your objects of worship, I even found an altar..." Wait a minute. Paul was walking around where? Looking at what? Remember, this was a culture where temple prostitution was rampant. If we are supposed to abstain from every appearance of evil, what was Paul doing in a place of idols? Just how carefully was he looking, anyway?

Paul gives us an example of observing a culture—all of it— the good side, the bad side, the bright spots, the darkness. As he observed, he was making mental notes: What is important to these people? How do they spend their time? How do they think? What would they say their life is lacking? How do they entertain themselves? What are their hungers? How much do they know about the true God? Paul was looking for connections—for windows and doorways for the message of a God who sent his Son to die and rise from the dead to form an eternal group of followers. Paul found what he was looking for in two places: in their pagan places of worship and in their art. He discovered an unknown god he could identify for them and a poem through which he could affirm God's nearness: "As some of your own poets have said, 'We are his offspring'" (Acts 17:28).

As a student of his culture, of its religious and social practices, of its political life, Paul found truth everywhere. He became as knowledgeable as he could about the culture of the people he wanted to reach.

4   *Conclusion*

Ten Times Better

I am reminded of the Old Testament story about Daniel and his three friends who, because of their wisdom and knowledge, rose to prominent positions serving the king of a pagan empire. "To these four young men God gave knowledge and understanding of all kinds of literature and learning" (Dn 1:17, italics mine). The implication is that they had "secular" knowledge as well as spiritual knowledge of God. They were well acquainted with all kinds of information and knowledge that any intelligent person of their day would understand and could dialogue in the cultural marketplace of ideas and influence. "In every matter of wisdom and understanding about which the king questioned them, he found them ten times better than all the magicians and enchanters in his whole kingdom" (v. 20).

Of course, not every person is asked to be this knowledgeable. The important thing about these men is that someone who knew God was so well informed. And in their knowledge and understanding, nothing appeared to be off limits. They knew everything the evil enchanters of the kingdom knew times ten. Their God was so big, and their fear of anyone or anything else was so small, that they could learn about the world and also be full of faith.

We need to be good students of the world. We need to be aware of what the world is thinking, what it is looking for, and what it is worshiping. We need to be looking for opportunities to put a name on the unknown god that the world is worshiping in ignorance, and let them know, to their great surprise and joy, that he is no longer unknown.

SIX

Saints Too Soon

Paradoxically, what intrudes between God and human beings is our fastidious morality and pseudo-piety. It is not the prostitutes and tax-collectors who find it most difficult to repent.[1]

BRENNAN MANNING

1   *What We Are Doing Wrong*

Testimony Time

The world is not wrong as much as it is lost, and we Christians may be wrong more than we know. Our unyielding hold on our own self-righteousness and self-proclaimed superiority keeps us from effectively representing the gospel of Jesus Christ in the world. We do not see ourselves accurately. For too long, we have tried to draw people to Christ by showcasing our rightness, when all along the good news of Christ's forgiveness of our wrongness is the real message.

The degree to which we feel removed from sin and sinners is the degree to which we will render ourselves ineffective for the gospel. We come from a long tradition of thinking that our impeccable lives will be the gospel's most treasured possession, and that by nature of our glowing brilliance we will draw the world to us. As it turns out, we are the ones who treasure those perfect lives. The only treasure of sinners is the gospel. When we see ourselves as saints too soon, we leave the point of the gospel behind, forgetting why it is such good news.

For as long as I can remember, Christians have held the false belief that the greatest witness we have in the world is our caliber of life—the things we do or don't do that set us apart from the world. By being different, we are somehow supposed to make everyone stop dead in their tracks and want to be like us. I can still hear the sermons from my childhood about people in the world—sad, unfortunate folks—falling all over themselves for an opportunity to be like me and have what I have because I'm a Christian. I'm still surprised sometimes when they don't.

If I wasn't traveling extensively visiting Christian college campuses and talking with students, I would have thought that this witness by legalism was a thing of the past—something my generation shed when our neat little Christian lives met the reality of sin, struggle, and doubt—certainly not a legalism we would pass on to our children. This is not the case. I am baffled at how prevalent this notion is among Christian young people today and how vehemently they try to defend it when questioned. "How will the world know that we're different if we listen to the same music and watch the same movies that they do? How will they know that we're different if we show up at the same places?" Their questions demonstrate the strength of this thinking. Every generation struggles with what Brennan Manning calls "my resident pharisee"[2]—that propensity toward good appearances that shields us from seeing our own sin or any connecting with other sinners. In the Christian circles I am familiar with, "my testimony" has always been synonymous with "my best foot forward."

The way evangelicals have come to use the word "testimony" says a great deal about how we think we will affect the world. In dictionary format, it looks like this:

testimony n. (pl. -ies) **1** verbal assent to the doctrines of the Christian faith. **2** declaration or statement of how one became a Christian, focusing especially on how bad they were before (the more details, the better) and how good they are now. **3** the impression a Christian makes on someone resulting in that person wanting or not wanting to be a Christian, depending on whether the impression was good or bad. **4** a deterrent to sin, as in: "Don't do such and such, it will ruin your testimony," or: "Remember what happened to so and so? He used to have a good testimony."

These errant definitions provide a field day for every pharisaical demon ever assigned to Christians. However you explain this or try to soft-pedal it to make it sound religious or even biblical, this sterling-behavior-wins-people-to-Christ model is flawed from the start. It sanctions pride, in that a Christian's greatest witness is a life better than everyone else's. We accomplish this by separating ourselves and making up rules we can abide by, so we can assure ourselves of being holier than those who don't follow the rules, even if they haven't heard what the rules are.

The power for this lie is that we get to control "the wonderful things God is doing in our lives," in essence, they are not things God is doing for us as much as they are things we are professing to do for him. We are living a prescribed "holy" life based on a list of what we do and don't do. Of course, no one outside of our Christian circle cares about these things the way we do, which pushes non-Christians further outside our circle and makes them even less important to us. Giving our testimony amounts to telling how fortunate we are to not be like everyone else. It's not what God has done for us as much as how lucky he is to have us making a difference for him in the world. Thus, when we tell people what wonderful things God is doing for us by how different we are, we are never really vulnerable to God or anyone else. Good Christians never lose control of their image, because their image *is* their testimony and they have to maintain its polish.

In his famous *Screwtape Letters*, C.S. Lewis has Screwtape instructing the demon Wormwood on the nuances of leading his Christian subject into this kind of thinking:

> You must teach him to mistake this contrast between the circle that delights and the circle that bores him for the contrast between Christians and unbelievers. He must be made to feel (he'd better not put it into words) "how different we Christians

are"; and by "we Christians" he must really, but unknowingly, mean "my set"; and by "my set" he must mean not "the people who, in their charity and humility, have accepted me," but "the people with whom I associate by right."[3]

But this approach to evangelism has never worked. This is not to be confused with the impact of a real change effected by the Holy Spirit. Genuine change happens to us and through us with no respect for our attempts to produce it or hide it.

My parents constantly reminded me as a child that my older sister was able to share her testimony with her eighth grade class because she refused to participate in the social dances at school. As a result I carried a note from my parents excusing me from similar school dances from the fifth grade on.

Unfortunately, I never got the opportunity to share my faith with my classes, nor did I ever understand why my faith stipulated that I not dance. I just stood apart. This practice had nothing to do with spirituality; it had everything to do with being different. It seems to me now that this difference could have been anything. It could have been: Christians don't do math on Wednesdays or Christians don't get driver's licenses until they're eighteen or Christians tuck in their shirts even when it's cool not to. It was simply a way of standing out from the crowd, to which we attached spiritual significance and no small amount of spiritual pride. Whatever made us different meant we were better in some recognizable way.

This testimony by dissimilarity is a rewrite of the Scriptures:

By this shall all men know that you are my disciples,
by the music you don't listen to,
by the movies you don't watch,
by the beverages you don't drink,

by the dances you don't participate in,
by the stand you take on all of these things, and mostly
by your impeachable, impeccable conduct.

The question no one ever asked was, "Who cares?" We know the world doesn't, because these things are not important to them. Or, if they are, it's for different reasons. For instance, plenty of non-Christians don't drink. Is that supposed to make everyone want to know what's different about them? It's their choice if they don't want to drink in this postmodern world of countless choices. No one even bothers to ask.

I figured it out the other day. Christians are the only ones who care about this. Those testimonies we gave that were supposed to change the world? Well, we were in church when we gave them, talking to people who already believed. The world wasn't there to hear us. We were talking to each other, telling each other how important it was to be different and finding comfort in being able to clearly define our differences.

2   *True Testimony*

The Muddy Hands of God

There's a story in the New Testament that helps to identify what a real testimony is. It took place when Jesus healed a man who had been blind from birth, by making mud with dirt and his own saliva and putting it on the man's eyes. He then told the man to go wash in the pool; when he returned, he could see. Later, the Pharisees tried to question him about what had happened to him because, being good Pharisees, they were upset that Jesus had done this on the Sabbath. Making mudpies was obviously not proper sabbatical behavior.

Therefore the Pharisees also asked him how he had received his sight. "He put mud on my eyes," the man replied, "and I washed, and now I see."

Some of the Pharisees said, "This man [Jesus] is not from God, for he does not keep the Sabbath."

But others asked, "How can a sinner do such miraculous signs?" So they were divided.

Finally they turned again to the blind man, "What have you to say about him? It was your eyes he opened."

The man replied, "He is a prophet."

The Jews still did not believe that he had been blind and had received his sight until they sent for the man's parents. "Is this your son?" they asked. "Is this the one you say was born blind? How is it that now he can see?"

"We know he is our son," the parents answered, "and we know he was born blind. But how he can see now, or who opened his eyes, we don't know. Ask him. He is of age; he will speak for himself..."

A second time they summoned the man who had been blind. "Give glory to God," they said. "We know this man is a sinner."

He replied, "Whether he is a sinner or not, I don't know. One thing I do know. I was blind but now I see!"   JOHN 9:13-25

This, in its simplest form, is the essence of a testimony. *"I was blind but now I see. Something happened to me. I am not an expert on theology; I just know that I am not the same man I was yesterday. My life has been altered. I can see now where I couldn't before. I can't even tell you a whole lot about the guy who did it, except he had to have been from God, because what happened to me was a miracle and only God can do miracles."*

A testimony tells something that happened to us. It witnesses to a power greater than ourselves. The speaker is humbled when talking about how God met an inner need or desperation. *"He touched me. He put mud on my eyes and told me to go wash and when I did, I could see. You go figure. I don't get it either. I just know that I was blind and now I can see."*

This man was no religious expert, but in the matter of a real encounter with God, he surpassed the Pharisees: They had been studying God all their lives and never had an encounter like this. The muddy hands of God touched this man in an intimate and powerful way. He gave expert testimony, a testimony which had nothing to do with his behavior. It had nothing to do with being different. It had everything to do with being touched by God. That is expert testimony.

When Jesus said, "You will be my witnesses" (Acts 1:8), he was not talking about behavior. He was talking about how he was no longer going to be around and now needed his disciples to bear witness that he had been among them and tell what he had accomplished while he was there. A witness was simply someone who saw something. A *good* witness had a good view of what happened. In this light, the best witnesses were most likely the people who were the most poorly behaved or the most unfortunate—the prostitutes and tax-collectors and lepers and demon-possessed. They got the closest view of Jesus, such as the woman with an issue of blood who managed by faith to touch his garment in a crowd and experience the power of his healing strength flow through her body. Or the leper who was touched and healed by Jesus, even though he was a proclaimed "untouchable." These were the best witnesses for Christ. The poor witnesses were the ones who didn't have a good view of what really happened like the Pharisees and Sadducees and leaders of the synagogues. The worst witnesses were those who never had a life-changing encounter with Jesus.

The Greatest Sinner

We've spent the better part of a century trying to show the world how different we are as Christians. We now have some catching up to do in the reality department. Our behavior as the spiritually elite obstructs our message.

Most non-Christians see Christians as a bunch of goody-two-shoes who look down our noses at the rest of the world. Where do you suppose they got this idea? Maybe it was all that spiritual posturing we did for the sake of our testimonies. Well, our testimonies have backfired on us. By convincing the world that we were different, we only succeeded in convincing many of them that they do not want to have anything to do with us. We may have impressed each other, but we didn't impress the world.

We've said that the gospel is for everyone, but we've acted as if it were just for us. We've cut ourselves off from that which makes us common with the rest of the world. Christians have cultivated an image that has nothing to do with sin and, thus, nothing to do with sinners. We have distanced ourselves from the world and taken on a form of spiritual pride. It's a sad day for the gospel when it is seen as good news only for good people.

For the sake of the gospel, it is time to show the world how very much the same we are. It's time to join Paul on the "worst of sinners" list. Yes, the Apostle Paul would put himself right in the middle of the world for which Christ died. In fact, he felt he was *more* of a sinner than the next guy, and less deserving of God's grace than any one. "Here is a trustworthy saying that deserves full acceptance: Christ Jesus came into the world to save sinners—of whom I am the worst" (1 Tm 1:15). Sounds like Paul is at an Alcoholics Anonymous meeting, doesn't it? "Hi, guys, I'm Paul and I'm a sinner—the worst"—a claim that would have been con-tested by other members present, convinced of their own bent to sinning.

Every believer should be absolutely convinced, beyond the shadow of a doubt, of being the worst sinner on the face of the earth. Worst there is, was, and ever will be. No contest. And if this is not the case, if there is any inkling of a thought that somebody out there might be worse than I am, then there is reason to believe that I have not yet done adequate business with God about my own sin.

The great hymnwriters thought this way. Their salvation con-tinually astonished them. Our hymnals portray their amazement. Consider lines like, "Amazing love! how can it be that Thou, my God, shouldst die for me!" No, this is not merely "die for me," as in a theological doctrine, this is "die for *me*," as in wonder that out of all the people in the world, he would have included *me*—in this case, Charles Wesley—the worst of the lot. Phillip Bliss, another hymnwriter, makes it even clearer when he concludes that "Jesus loves even me." There's a wealth of meaning in that one word "even." *Even* me, the lowest, the least deserving, the worst. Or, Charles Wesley again, this time writing, "'Tis mercy all, immense and free, for, O my God, it found out *me*!" His implica-tion is, "God's mercy had to look really hard because I was a long way off!"

These hymnwriters placed themselves in a camp with the world. Yes, they were saved out of the world, but they never left it and never forgot who they were without Christ. I believe this is what Paul meant when he said, "I *am* the worst"—present tense. He knew himself. He knew one thing separated him from the next guy: Jesus Christ and his death on Paul's behalf. The next guy either didn't know yet, or didn't get it. Either way, Jesus was the only difference.

One of Them

How this perspective changes our view of the world! Suddenly the world is full of other sinful people like us, for whom Christ died, and our job is to tell the good news to as many as possible. "God isn't mad at us anymore. He took it out on Jesus. Believe Jesus and you'll be forgiven, washed clean, as if all that stuff you did never happened! Come on, guys, this is good news—too good to be true." This perspective says Christ died for "US." No more Christ died for "them."

When I discovered I was one of "them," I entered the kingdom of heaven. Yes, earlier in my life I "said the words" and "prayed the prayer," but my thinking about myself and the world was skewed. I was "OK" because I was on the inside. The words and the prayer were an initiation into a group to which I already belonged. As in the words of Screwtape, "The great thing (for the kingdom of Satan) is to make Christianity a mystery religion in which he (the believer) feels himself one of the initiates."[4] When I finally saw myself as the worst of sinners—as one of the sinners I used to condemn—the gospel made sense. Up until then, I didn't understand why Christ died.

I sometimes imagine this scene: I'm sitting down to eat at the marriage supper of the Lamb and look across the table at some scoundrel I never suspected to see there. "How did you get here?" I will say, to which he will reply, "Same way you did, friend."

I Can See Clearly Now

Too often Christians try to take out the speck in the world's eye, ignoring the plank in our own. "Hold still," we say. "You've got something in your eye. Here, let me get it out."

"Yikes! Get away from me!" says the world. "What is that I see sticking out of *your* eye? You're gonna hit me with that thing!"

"You hypocrite," says Jesus to the one passing judgment. "First take the plank out of your own eye, and then you will see clearly to remove the speck from your brother's eye" (Mt 7:5).

There's a plank in my eye? No wonder it's so hard to see. No wonder every time I try to help someone I end up hurting them. When we pass judgment, it's always harder on us than on the one being judged. Most of the time they don't even know we're judging them, but we know when it all comes back on us. Jesus said, "For in the same way you judge others, you will be judged, and with the measure you use, it will be measured to you" (Mt 7:2). Imagine the judgment one person is capable of heaping on the world all coming back on him!

Take a moment to make a mental list of the most heinous sins you can think of. What did you read about in the paper this morning that raised the hair on the back of your neck? What was on the news that made you wish you had never heard it? What did that politician do that got your goat? Now write down next to each of these sins, "Speck." Next make a mental list of your own sins. Be ruthless. Put down the slightest, the most insignificant or private ones you think don't hurt anybody. The casual ones. The sins of omission. Now write next to each one, "Plank." This is what Jesus is getting at. The issue is not which sin is worse; it's which sin is *mine*. Mine are always worse because they are mine.

No matter how bad the other guy's sins are, mine are worse. This is true regardless of the weightiness of the sins involved. The other's will always be a speck; mine will always be a plank. But there is hope and redemption in this story as well. I can do something—I can remove my plank. Then I will be able to see clearly and compassionately. I'll say, *"Hey, buddy, you've got a speck in your eye? That's nothing. You should have seen what I just pulled out of mine!"*

It's wonderful to be released from judgment, to be just another forgiven sinner, after trying to be a good testimony all your life. I once heard a woman put this feeling appropriately into the words of a popular song: "I can see clearly now the *log* is gone." The celebratory nature of that song is entirely appropriate.

When I was a kid attending Christian camp, we used to end the week with what was then called—and this is the truth—a fagot service. This name came from an English word which means "a bundle of sticks or twigs bound together as fuel." The service consisted of a fellowship time outdoors around a campfire where campers would take a stick from the bundle, throw it on the fire, and give their "testimony." When I reached high school, my peers and I knew that a similar word was used as a derogatory reference to a male homosexual. Every time someone mentioned a "fagot service" we snickered. In my mind now this scene is thick with the rank irony of throwing a "fagot" on the fire of our glowing spiritual testimonies while bundles of sticks clogged our eyes.

Let's institute a new service, fueled not by the sticks of judgment, but by the planks pulled from our own eyes. Let's turn away from the fire and with clear eyes embrace a world full of people we once condemned. Christians can bring healing in society—but only when our eyes are clear of judgment and prejudice; when we see everyone as someone for whom Christ died, when we treat every person, no matter how sinful, as one who might be in the process of being saved; and when we remember that we are "the worst of sinners."

3   *Conclusion*

Saved Sinners

There are only two kinds of people in the world: sinners who know they're forgiven, and those who don't yet know. Jesus already forgave everybody. He finished that on the cross. We can identify with the world because we are nothing more than sinners who have accepted his sacrifice in our place. The world needs to hear this from us. Most people don't have a clue that this is what Christianity is all about.

We need to give the world a more realistic presentation of ourselves—we've been scaring them away for too long with self-imposed images of our saintliness. The world has always been more ready to hear the astonished witness of a saved sinner than the calculated piety of a holy saint. I rather like the Catholic way of looking at sainthood. It's hard to get in—you have to die first. Whether you take that figuratively or literally, it's a good point.

It's most important that we see ourselves honestly, that we view the world through plank-less eyes. We should never be far away from full awareness of what we would be without Christ.

> And from my smitten heart with tears,
> Two wonders I confess—
> The wonder of redeeming love
> And my unworthiness.[5]
> ELIZABETH C. CLEPHANE

SEVEN

Letter to the Postmodern Church

Civility is... a willingness to promote
the well-being of people who are very
different, including people who seriously
disagree with you on important matters.[1]
RICHARD MOUW

1   *Doing Good in the World*

Peter's World and Ours

The first epistle of Peter might just as well be named *Letter to the Postmodern Church,* for it describes believers of that day as "strangers in the world" and "scattered" throughout the region. These words have great relevance to our own time.

The early church was scattered throughout Asia because of the persecution of the Christians. But our fragmented society is "scattered" as well, by the breakdown of family and social structure. No one feels a part of the whole anymore. No one can find it. There was a time when *Our Town* was everybody's town. But Thornton Wilder died and our town was hit by the bomb of global technology and multiculturalism; now, various ethnic, racial, religious groups, and social strata lie scattered around society like smoldering shrapnel. No longer can we call any town ours, only parts of town, like China Town, Japan Town, Korea Town, South Central LA, Westwood... each with its own cultural identity, each a world away from the next. And the barriers no longer divide only ethnic neighborhoods. Now "our town" is the small ethnic, social, religious, political, or ideological group we belong to.

Even though Peter is talking about Christians as strangers in the world and temporary aliens from a heavenly kingdom, it's as if everyone is a stranger now. The world borders on overpopulation and yet we are all strangers to each other. We pass through public places crowded with humanity and remain alone. In many ways we are strangers even to ourselves.

Our world is similar to the one that received Peter's letter; in both worlds Christians are maligned by society. Peter was sensitive to the reputation of Christians. If they suffered and were criticized, he wanted to make sure it was for the right reasons. As much as possible, he wanted to silence criticism with good deeds that benefited society. Peter's concerns were for the sake of the gospel—that it might be central in the lives of the believers, and that everything they did might bode well for the gospel.

The themes of his letter relate directly to our own social and cultural needs. In Peter's world and ours, words are not as important as actions; the gospel lived means as much if not more than the gospel proclaimed, and good deeds have to speak for themselves.

"Therefore, prepare your minds for action..." (1 Pt 1:13), and we are reminded again of the necessity of using our minds. And yet our minds are not for thinking only; they are also for action. Peter wants to send Christians off into a fragmented society with their minds set on doing good. The centrality of this positive activity in the world is impossible to miss. Throughout Peter's letter, we can hear echoes of Jesus' words: "Let your light shine before men, that they may see your good deeds and praise your Father in heaven" (Jn 5:16). Listen to Peter:

Live such good lives among the pagans that, though they accuse you of doing wrong, they may see your good deeds and glorify God (2:12). For it is God's will that by doing good you should silence the ignorant talk of foolish men (2:15). Who is going to harm you if you are eager to do good? (3:13)... keeping a clear conscience, so that those who speak maliciously of your good behavior in Christ may be ashamed of their slander (3:16).

Peter sought a reputation that turns critics into those who glorify God.

They Shoot Doctors, Don't They?

The church today desperately needs a new paradigm for its presence in the world, and one has been in Peter's letter to the churches for nearly two thousand years. If Peter observed the Christian subculture in America, I'm afraid he would find merely one more piece of shrapnel glowing in its moral indignation. Far from actually being in the world, the Christian subculture is not touching any more than the fringes of its own well-guarded borders. Peter would say, "Break camp, crawl over the wall of your subculture, out past the friendly fire, and start doing good in the world. God will take care of the war; you get out there and start helping and loving the casualties on all sides of battle, because you do not wrestle with flesh and blood enemies of God (see Ephesians 6:12).

So many Christians today have assumed a hostile stance against the world in the name of spiritual warfare. They have taken up arms politically and are trying to influence society to change. A man on a Christian talk show pointed out that we are not only the light of the world but also the salt of the earth. He went on to say that salt is a preservative, and we should try to preserve what once made this country great. But does that mean we churn out salt in large quantities wherever we feel it is needed? Does that mean that we boycott and demonstrate and organize politically? Is our saltiness in society something we consciously rub in the wounds of those we don't like? Do we salt down the very ones we are trying to reach with the love of Christ?

Rebecca Manley Pippert wrote a very insightful book on evangelism several years ago called *Out of the Salt Shaker and Into the World*. Her idea was for us to spread out in society and not huddle in the safety of our Christian "salt shaker" subculture. So what have we done now? Well, we've taken the admonition to get involved all right; it's just that someone played a trick on us like my kids do sometimes with the salt shaker—they unscrew the top and set it loosely on the shaker. We dump "our salt" on society all at once and ruin everyone's taste.

To listen to Christian talk radio these days is to hear a great deal of outrage from Christians trying to gain lost cultural ground by playing the part of the angry minority. Themes against abortion, gay rights, sex education, and the outlawing of prayer in schools dominate the Christian airwaves. Some Christians acting as the moral arm of society are trying to wage war in the legislative halls of Washington and the front doors of abortion clinics, instead of in the heavenly realms where Paul put the battle (see Eph 6:12). We misuse Scripture when we use the language of spiritual warfare in the context of social morality. These open appeals to resentment and warfare without a spiritual context and sound teaching are extremely dangerous to the Christian body. They incite attitudes that are far from the forgiveness that Christ exhibited on the cross.

As a guest on a recent talk show, I lamented the negative characterization of Christians by non-Christians. A woman called in and raised the abortion issue. Was I saying that we should stand by while babies are being slaughtered? In the name of Christ, shouldn't we do something? Yes, abortion is a travesty, but is the stopping of abortions what we want to be known for in the world? Is it the hill we are willing to die on? Did God decide this was to be the major issue for Christians in the 1990s, or did we? These emotional issues skirt the big question. Are we to preserve the moral elements in society at the risk of alienating unbelievers for whom Christ died? If by banding together and fighting abortion, Christians are at the same time turning off a host of non-Christians to the only source from which they can hear the gospel, we may save some babies, but lose a generation. It's the age-old nearsightedness of winning a battle only to find out that we have lost the war.

Yes, these moral issues are important and we all do have a God-given responsibility to stand up for what is right and just in society. But when all is said and done, do we really want to be known as the generation who sold our birthright as bearers of the good news of Jesus Christ for a pot of political porridge?

Peter said do good in the world so that no one can bring a charge against you. Doesn't that mean we should be known as those who provide homes and support for mothers who choose to keep their babies? Believe it or not, the gospel lived out by men and women who are known for their love is more important than the abortion issue.

Christians who believe there is a simple political solution to every social problem are mistaken. John Seel points this out in a comment that is worth quoting in its entirety.

Majority status—demographic size—never translates into cultural power... The popular fallacy has been that by large numbers and political legislation we can bring culture back to its original Judeo-Christian heritage. That's been the assumption. The truth of the matter is: culture is pre-political—that behind all the political legislation are the habits of the heart that give people the dispositions to follow any particular legislation. Without people's dispositions to follow particular laws, they won't follow them. Laws become just "parchment barriers," to quote James Madison. So the truth of the matter is, we need a greater attention on the cultural arena—that is—the crisis today is not political; it's not economic; the crisis today is cultural. It has to do with the beliefs and values of Americans and those within the church. The problem evangelicals have had is they don't understand how culture is in fact shaped. They've assumed that it is shaped the same way politics is. Not so... We're fighting an upstream battle without the kind of understanding of what, in fact, changes society. Boycotts and pickets and protests and demonstrations finally will not do.[2]

Into this volatile minefield, the words of Peter come again with a sensibility and gentleness that drives away wrath, "Who can harm you if you are eager to do good?" (see 3:13). This is the focus Peter wants us to have in the world. He's not talking as much about *being* good as he is about *doing* good. The list of good deeds is long and varied, because it includes going the extra mile at work to serving in a soup kitchen.

Our Town

In a fragmented society where not everyone speaks the same language, everyone understands a message of loving service. A cup of cold water offered in the name of Jesus needs no translation. Peter wanted Christians in Galatia, Cappadocia, Asia, and Bithynia to have a reputation for making their towns better places in which to live. That point was to silence the critics of the gospel by the contributions Christians were making in their communities.

What if a businessman criticized Christians and then found out that the Little League coach who spent extra time instilling confidence in his son was a Christian? What if a social activist condemned Christians but kept running into them working overtime at the social agencies in town? What if a working mother put down Christians and then found that her children's favorite schoolteacher was a Christian? What if a homosexual spent his whole life bashing Christians, and then discovered that one of them visits him regularly, now that he's dying with AIDS? What if a CEO tried to put down Christians, and then discovered a respected leader in the Chamber of Commerce is a Christian and a noted philanthropist in the community?

Peter wants Christians to have a reputation that lends credibility to the gospel. He wants them to be not only bearers of the gospel but doers of good deeds, so that nothing will stand in the way of the message of the gospel. "Who is going to harm you if you are eager to do good?" (1 Pt 3:13).

2   *The Preeminence of the Gospel*

Whose Reputation?

Peter's ultimate concern is for the gospel of Jesus Christ. He is interested in the Christian's reputation insofar as it gives a greater chance for the gospel to be heard. One's personal reputation is only a means to the end of putting the gospel in the best possible light.

The current activity of some Christians does not seem to manifest a concern for the preeminence of the gospel message. Other agendas, such as social morality and personal safety, are presently pushing the gospel into the background. In many cases Christians are actually garnering a bad name for themselves, and this is reflecting negatively on the gospel.

The gospel of Jesus Christ is all about saving the lost. When any agenda becomes more important than this, we are really saying that something else is more important than people perishing eternally. Nothing is *that* important. We are representatives of Christ, Christ's ambassadors, in fact, "as though God were making his appeal through us" (2 Cor 5:20). If we are turning off the world through an antagonistic attitude, we are cutting off their primary access to God. This is not just a matter of priorities; we are talking about the eternal destiny of the souls of men, women, and children, and our responsibility as stewards of the good news of Jesus Christ.

We need to do something to redeem our reputation in the world right now, because it is not good; and whenever the reputation of Christians suffers, the gospel suffers. What can we do? Peter has told us. Get out into the world and do good.

Jesus Has Left the Building

It is becoming increasingly obvious that the Christian subculture is often counterproductive to the gospel. Our crosses and fish symbols and bumper stickers and buttons, once an attempt to identify with Christ in society, have now become an identification with causes that many find objectionable. As far as the world is concerned, Christians no longer represent Christ. They stand for prayer in schools, capital punishment, the right to bear arms, censorship in the arts, television control, and parental warnings on rap and rock music. They'll stand against abortion, gay rights, and AIDS funding. While these things are important to many, they have become identified with the Christian cause to such an extent that the world thinks we have discovered a way to make our own will be done on earth, as we believe it is done in heaven.

Through their presence in the media, leading Christian organizations in America enjoy power and influence in society and government as never before. I can still hear the words of my twenty-five-year-old visions and dreams, "Imagine how we could spread the gospel if we had such-and-such resources." Well, we have those resources now, but something happened to the perceived importance of the gospel in the process of gaining control of them. Now it doesn't appear to be the gospel that we are spreading as much as our own view of how we want the world to be.

If I know Jesus, he's already "left the building" of the Christian subculture. We had our fifteen minutes of fame (ala Andy Warhol) and now there's other work to be done. This is the way it is with Jesus—he's outside the camp. He's in the world seeking someone who will represent his cause. God did not send his Son into the world to condemn the world, but that the world through him might be saved (see Jn 3:17). If the Christian subculture exists primarily to condemn the world, you can be sure that Jesus is not having any part of it.

Let's care for the world the way Jesus does. He cares for the whole person. He healed all who came to him and didn't ask them first if they were going to stick around for the sermon. He didn't heal people merely to get their attention; he was concerned about each person as someone made in his image. I don't believe he asked them first if they planned on becoming a part of his team or checked out their moral and political leanings. He simply healed them because he was moved with compassion over their pain. What if they never accepted his message of salvation, and all Jesus gave them was a few more days, weeks, months, or years of life before they ultimately died, some of them still in their sins? Was it important to Christ to improve their life for a few "worthless" moments? Apparently so.

In her beautiful hymn, "Rescue the Perishing," Fanny Crosby has captured the heart of the Christian toward unbelievers. We would do well to check our attitude with the one she represents here. Perhaps it would be fitting to think of someone dying of AIDS as you look over these words. It's almost as if she knew...

Rescue the perishing, care for the dying,
Snatch them in pity from sin and the grave;
Weep o'er the erring one, lift up the fallen,
Tell them of Jesus, the mighty to save.

Though they are slighting Him, still He is waiting,
Waiting the penitent child to receive;
Plead with them earnestly, plead with them gently,
He will forgive if they only believe.

Down in the human heart, crushed by the tempter,
Feelings lie buried that grace can restore;
Touched by a loving heart, wakened by kindness,
Cords that are broken will vibrate once more.

Rescue the perishing, care for the dying;
Jesus is merciful, Jesus will save.

3   *What the World Needs to See*

What the World Needs Now...

Good deeds done in the world were important to Peter because they were important to Jesus. But what will these good deeds look like? They may look like anybody else's good deeds, actually. Christians aren't the only ones capable of doing good in the world. In many cases, we need to join up with non-Christians who are already doing good. Many community organizations link services with people, but they need more volunteers and more money. Christians working alongside non-Christians in serving the poor and the homeless, the abused and the battered, will have an opportunity to serve those they are working with as well as those in need. Many times the workers are as needy as those they are serving, especially those who are constantly tending to the sick and dying.

Christians who work to serve the needs of the world share a common grace with non-Christians. God has allowed even those who don't love him to experience love. It is in this common giving and receiving that the gospel can be shared. It is what someone called one beggar showing another beggar where to find food.

Christians need to care about their communities through the Parent Teachers Association, community action groups, sports and recreation programs, the chamber of commerce, and as contributors to the arts—filling positions from workers to board members with those who know and love Jesus Christ. As Christians, we belong to both a heavenly and an earthly kingdom, and it will be our commitment to the earthly one that will give us opportunity to introduce people to the heavenly kingdom.

Christians need to care about the global environment. For the sake of the gospel we need to be concerned about the forces that threaten and endanger life on this planet. No matter how fallen, this is still our Father's world. He takes personal time with every plant and tree and animal and he knows when a sparrow falls, so you can be sure he sees the delicate rain forests being ravaged, and the air in our crowded cities being polluted and the ability of land to give back its wealth being destroyed by lack of crop rotation. By caring about our environment, we send a message to the world that God cares about his world and has made us all responsible for it.

Christians need to be involved in politics, not a "Christian politic" but Christians as Republicans and Democrats and Independents acting out their convictions through the existing political system.

Christians need to work in all areas of the arts, not doing Christian art but being Christians in the arts. In forming a subculture, Christians have created a sympathetic, less critical audience. It's time to get out of our subculture where so much is assumed, and become artists who must struggle with our faith, the message and the art form, and an audience that does not presume belief. The challenge will sharpen our faith and our ability to articulate it. The world needs Christians in television. The world needs Christians writing in its newspapers, its commentaries. The world needs Christians writing its plays and its novels. The world needs to hear a Christian voice from out of its own marketplace.

The Third Wave of Philanthropy

Peter Berger calls what is needed in society the third wave of philanthropy. Bob Buford calls it Leadership Network, an organization he formed of "social entrepreneurs"—men and women who want to convert the energy they used building businesses and careers into building social initiatives that originate from their Christian motivation to be salt and light in the world.

Take Tom Luce, for example. A Texas attorney and former candidate for governor with a passion for education, he has formed "Just for the Kids," a nonprofit, nonpartisan, grassroots foundation dedicated to providing the children of his state the opportunity to receive a better public education. "As we continue to moralize about the demise of the family, sex education, TV violence, latchkey kids and other sidebar issues, another school year has passed and more kids have fallen behind."[3] Tom's organization brings together school administrators, legislators, and the private sector to energize struggling schools, enhance their resources, aid parents, and provide tutorial help to bring kids up to speed.

What's important to Tom Luce? The fact that 78 percent of the children in the Dallas Independent School District are not able to read at their grade level. A case could probably be made that this degeneration of the public schools is due at least in part to the shift of many Christian families to private schools and home schooling. And here is the irony of a Christian going back into the world to benefit the lives of children whom other Christians in the name of morality and in fear of the world have abandoned. In the process, Tom is rebuilding a reputation for the gospel by offering something of substance to the community.

A similar concern moved Duncan Campbell, a Christian businessman who owned a timber investment firm in Portland, Oregon, to create Friends of the Children, a mentoring program for high risk kids in the Portland area. His organization employs gifted adults to serve as mentors, tutors, coaches, advocates, and friends of kids who have been abandoned or who are missing support at home. Duncan Campbell is a social entrepreneur and a member of Bob Buford's network of Christian leaders with a new eye on philanthropy which involves more than just writing checks.

The members of this network transfer their business expertise to the charitable sector. They have made a pact with each other to commit themselves to four criteria: a focused vision with clear outcomes, a minimum of one full-time staff person, a personal monetary investment of at least $100,000, and a commitment of at least 30 percent of their personal time and energy to the project they are creating.[4]

"These men and women are asking not what their entrepreneurial zeal can do for themselves, but what that zeal can achieve for the family of man."[5] This is how the secular press interpreted it in *The Dallas Morning News*. However, there is more to what drives these people.

Judy Williams remembers when she was pregnant with their first child and struggling to help her husband, Don, get through law school. Now as chairman of the board of the largest real estate company in the United States, Don Williams also serves as president of the Dallas Citizen's Council, that city's most prestigious and influential civic organization. He and Judy spend large amounts of time in civic service, primarily through a drug and alcohol abuse program they started called Dallas Challenge.

"We're near the end of politics as we know it," says Don Williams. "Americans are in a mood for less government. The tax base is exhausted and programs aren't working." And so Williams moved in to help fill in the gap.

> I'll go where others don't want to go. The people we ought to be the most helpful to are the people close by. We've overstated the importance of theology and understated the role of helpful serving.... As individuals, we are the product of a set of relationships—with God, with God's people, with the kingdom at large, our families, our neighborhoods, our business colleagues. And individual obligations begin with those relationships."[6]

Don and Judy see themselves serving, not only the family of God but also the family of mankind. "It's a form of service to community and of evangelism," he says. "It can lead someone to ask, 'What is it with you?' and that's when you can share your faith." This is what Peter would call giving "an answer to everyone who asks you to give the reason for the hope that you have" (1 Pt 3:15).

Of course, very few of us will have such financial resources or community influence, but we can all learn from their point of view. While so many Christians are leaving the world, these people are going back in with the love of Jesus, and they're not waiting for someone else to do it.

4   *Conclusion*

The Gospel According to Willie Nelson and Leon Russell

My neighbor was dying of cancer. He was the best neighbor anyone could have: He looked after our dogs and kept an eye on things when we were gone. His wife is a born-again Christian. She remembers a day when George was baptized and very involved in the church, but he never talked to me about that. In fact, George would deny that he was a Christian at all. As his physical condition worsened, his denials intensified.

Years ago, he had a pastor who deceived his congregation and embezzled money, including a large amount of George's hard-earned savings. Over the years, he let his bitterness fester until it choked out any ability to believe. My attempts to bring up anything about God or the gospel were met with vitriolic disgust. I thought perhaps he might soften as the end approached, but instead, he called Christianity a myth and even decried me as a fool for believing.

And then one day, I noticed that Willie Nelson and Leon Russell were going to do a concert at a local club not five minutes from my house. It was to be a repeat performance, since this same pair had received rave reviews there earlier in the year. I thought of George because I knew he was a Willie Nelson fan. I also thought of how special it would be to hear these two singer/songwriters in an informal dinner club setting, sharing their songs back and forth from a lifetime of familiar favorites. I asked George if he wanted to go with me and he was overwhelmed. Of course he would go! The tickets were expensive and I had to fight him off to keep him from paying. His pride made it hard for him to receive.

As the event approached, his condition worsened and yet his excitement for the concert grew. His wife told me at one point that she wondered if he was keeping himself alive for it. On the night of the event, he showed up at my front door, decked in a new outfit including cowboy boots and a headband. With his gaunt face and long gray hair that hadn't been cut since he found out he was terminal, he looked like Willie himself.

The real surprise came at the concert, when Willie and Leon did a string of gospel songs that seemed to never end. I can't even remember them all, but they included "Will the Circle Be Unbroken?" "I'll Fly Away," and "I Saw the Light"—each song communicating the gospel and talking about heaven and eternity. George took it all in quietly, and I sat there marveling at how a couple of old codgers on stage could get away with saying everything I wanted to tell George but couldn't.

I know he was touched by the songs because as he left that night he said, "Well, as the Christians say, guess I'll see you here, there, or in the air." These were the last words I heard him utter. And I firmly believe, based on his ability to say those words and on what his wife told me about his last few days, that we will in fact be "in the air" when I see him next.

God is present in our culture and can make an appearance when and where we least expect it; and sometimes all it takes is a simple act of kindness to break through the thickest wall.

Nobody makes a greater mistake than he who did nothing because he could only do a little.
EDMUND BURKE

EIGHT

A Reason for the Hope

Christianity has survived Christians
for two thousand years now, which
from my point of view is evidence
that maybe something is going on there.[1]
T-BONE BURNETT

1   *No Fear but God*

So Many Fears

More than one commentator remarked during the presidential primaries of 1996 that Pat Buchanan's only real threat to Bob Dole's Republican candidacy was his ability to tap into the middle class fears of American people. If there is one human emotion common to every aspect of society today, it is fear. In a fragmented world, people fear encroachment from all sides. Violent gang wars of the inner cities are a glaring picture of what is happening in a more covert way in society as a whole. No neighborhood is safe anymore. When a crazed gunman can walk into a grammar school gymnasium in a sleepy Scottish town and point-blank murder sixteen kindergartners and a teacher, anything can happen anywhere.

We live with close personal fears like loss of a job, and distant global fears like the collapse of world economy. Everyone knows that the next Great Depression will be worldwide in scope and the next world war will probably be the last. And who can push the button on a spray can without wondering if the hole in the ozone layer is going to tear open and melt the Arctic Circle and turn the planet into Waterworld, and it was our one last squirt of hair spray that did it?

A handgun debate currently rages. Many want to outlaw handguns to reduce crime and gang warfare. Those who oppose these restrictions want to be sure they can protect themselves. If the bad guys are going to have guns, they don't want to be caught without them either. But, who decides who the bad guys are? And, do we outlaw guns so only outlaws will have them? Or, do we let everybody have them, so we can all sit around with jumpy trigger fingers and feel "safe"? Neither alternative seems desirable; both provoke fear.

Nowhere does the fear hit closer to home, however, than in economics. Job security is a myth. Social security is no longer secure. Technology is changing the face of the world so fast that certain skills needed today may be obsolete tomorrow. Employers operate in a fluctuating free market system that can mean the addition of 30,000 jobs today or the collapse of their company tomorrow. The cover of Studs Terkel's book *The Great Divide* pictures an American flag pulling apart, with stripes going to one side and stars to the other. Society is coming apart at the seams. The rich are getting richer, the poor are getting poorer, and the bottom is dropping out of the middle. Most people feel as if they're falling.

No Fear

Into this world Peter speaks again with pointed clarity. "Do not fear what they fear; do not be frightened" (1 Pt 3:14). Who is the "they" if it isn't everybody? "Do not fear what they fear" means that the fears gripping society should not have the same effect on Christians. "So do not worry, saying 'What shall we eat?' or 'What shall we drink?' or 'What shall we wear?' For the pagans run after these things, and your heavenly Father knows that you need them" (Mt 6:31-32). In the face of so many fears, Christians need to believe these words of Jesus. Our heavenly Father knows our situation and will take care of us. We are not alone.

To the Christian today, "no fear" should be more than a logo for a line of clothes. It may just be the greatest testimony we can have in the world—*not* to be afraid. When everyone else is jockeying for position, full of stress, kowtowing for their jobs to evil people of influence, we have a heavenly Father who watches over us and knows what we need. We either believe this or we don't. If we don't, we're just as afraid as everybody else. As the legalistic do's and don'ts that once separated Christians from non-Christians are falling away, what is going to make us different? Could it be having peace in a world full of fear?

Once in a while a Christian is caught in the crossfire of violence and the world gets to see the reaction. Forgiveness, hope, and courage can show themselves when a Christian's life is placed in the crucible. The world doesn't understand how the victim of a personal crime can forgive the criminal. Some of the strongest witnesses for Christ in the first half of the 1990s have come out of tragedies like the riots in Los Angeles and the bombing in Oklahoma City, where the faith of ordinary Christians was on display. How we react in hardship is often more crucial than what we say in a time of ease.

To Save the World or Make It Safe?

Unfortunately, fear and anger are rampant in Christian circles today. We seem to be about even with the world when it comes to the fear quotient. Indeed, we're so afraid that we're mad. We've got clout now, and we're going to do something about it. We need to ask ourselves a few questions.

Do we want a moral society because we are genuinely concerned about the quality of life for every human being? Or, is it that a more moral society means a more *safe* society—safer for *us* to carry on *our* lives with less encroachment from the pagan element? If so, we are grossly misunderstanding the gospel. Jesus did not come to make the world *safe;* he came to *save* it, and there is a world of difference between the two. In our overwhelming desire to be safe, we have taken up the world's solutions and are losing our opportunity to bring the peace of God to the world through Christ.

I can almost hear Peter asking us where the gospel is in all of these concerns. What kind of reputation are we building in the world as Christians? Peter says not to fear what they fear, because he wants something different to be evident in our lives. If we take his advice and stop letting fear control our responses, we can become a positive force for peace in the world, instead of a negative force trying to fight evil wherever we find it and getting sucked into the culture wars. We are so busy *reacting to* the world that we have no time or vision for *acting in* the world.

Robert W. Jenson, Associate Director of the Center for Catholic and Evangelical Theology and co-editor of *Either Or: The Gospel or Neo-Paganism,* worries that in siding with various political action groups, the church has lost its vision and influence in society. Instead of being the voice of God speaking a transcendent message into culture, the church is merely one more special interest group among many.

> When the church has a political agenda, it's no different than the political agenda of the National Rifle Association, or the NEA. The church has its axe to grind, and the polity computes that interest along with the others.... If the society will no longer let us set the agenda, then we will say "Hurrah" for the agenda society has got by way of maintaining our social influence.

Mr. Jenson points out that this change in the church's relationship to culture—from speaking to culture from God's point of view to siding with culture as merely one more special interest group—has as its most disastrous result the loss of the church's true relationship to God.

> There's an elementary point that... the modern church spends its time dancing around. The church claims to know the true

God. Now if indeed the entity the church knows is the true God, it is the one God of the universe and therefore the church knows the one thing needful to be known about all things. To the extent that the church backs off from this claim... it also gives up the claim to know God, and transforms its own worship into a kind of idolatrous enterprise—a worship of something less than God.[2]

Our fearful desire for a safe world has taken us far away from our calling. The world will never be safe for Christians. Jesus promised: "I have told you these things, so that in me you may have peace. In the world you will have trouble. But take heart! I have overcome the world" (Jn 16:33). Some modern Christians consider this verse a call to arms. They hear only the last part of it—where he has overcome the world. *"If he has overcome the world then we can too!"* But they fail to realize that Jesus is speaking from the end of history. This is a future tense view of God's ultimate victory over sin and death and evil that should give us courage now. The present reality is the purpose of this statement—we *will* have trouble in this world, but in the midst of that trouble he, and only he, will be our peace. Any other peace is a false one that leads us away from our mission of love and into idolatrous liaisons.

2   *No Lord but Christ*

A Holy Infiltration

"Set apart." These two words have been and continue to be a source of confusion. As Christians we have historically separated ourselves from as much contact with the world as possible, thinking that this is what it means to be set apart: to not be where the world is or go where the world goes or give an appearance of having anything to do with the world, beyond what is absolutely necessary.

In chapter four we discussed how the word *sanctify* from Jesus's prayer in John 17 has to do with an internal separation. Peter follows the same course of thinking; after he tells us not to be frightened he says, "But in your hearts set apart Christ as Lord" (1 Pt 3:15). We are not to find relief from this frightening world by separating ourselves from it; rather, we are to keep the frightening world from ruling our hearts by letting Christ rule there instead. The separation happens inside of us, not outside. This is a much deeper, much more difficult alignment, because we must make it happen in our hearts while we are surrounded by a fearful world. No one knows this better than Peter himself, who walked on water when his eyes were fixed on Christ, and succumbed to the ominous surroundings and almost drowned when his eyes were on the storm.

It's easier to set ourselves apart than it is to set apart Christ as Lord in us, but this is how we can impact society from the inside. It will not happen through the combined strength of Christians banding together to control the world or its institutions, but by individuals taking up positions in the world with Christ as Lord in their hearts—a sort of holy infiltration. God does not want us ruling the world from a power base of worldly influence. He wants us in the world with his rule established in our hearts. As is often the case, we turn this inside out. We would like our subculture to be our control center from which we keep the world at bay and rule it at the same time. Christ wants the center of control to be in each one of us where *he* rules, while we are scattered out in the world like granules of salt.

Peter is talking about a different power base and a different center of control than much of the church is operating from right now. It is not our job to make Christ Lord of our society. The lordship of Christ over culture is something we hold in our hearts, and act out of, but not something we try and force on those around us. Christ is Lord over culture in our hearts and in the church, but not in Washington, or on the school board, or at work, or in the university classroom. He has not even sought that lordship himself. Christ seeks lordship in the hearts of believers. He will deal with the rest of the world later. There will come a time when every knee bows to him (see Phil 2:10); but right now, only our knees are familiar with this position.

The Lost Art of Persuasion

"Since, then, we know what it is to fear the Lord, we try to persuade men" (2 Cor 5:11). In Paul's argument, we discover what this generation of Christians has lost. We must reclaim the lost art of persuasion. Here is what the apostle was saying: "We fear the Lord. Others do not fear the Lord, but we try to persuade them." Paul even went on to say, "What we are is plain to God, and I hope it is plain to your conscience." In other words, I hope we have persuaded you too, but that's not a guarantee. He realized that the only ones he could persuade were those who wished to be persuaded. Thus, whenever he spoke in the world, he expected to have some who believed, some who wanted to hear more, and some who wanted to throw him out of town (see Acts 17:32-34).

We have lost our generation at this juncture. We have opted for the power of politics, trying to accomplish what only God can do, by becoming Lord in people's hearts. This is why, for the sake of the gospel, we must lay down the rhetoric of political power and pick up the art of persuasion. Persuasion is civil and gracious. It respects the mind of the other and does not force anything on anyone. In persuasion, the power goes into the argument, not at the person. It bears weight on a person only if the argument is weighty and the individual is open enough to hear it. It is the truth, well articulated by believers who are already in the market-place, that should weigh on the souls of men and women, not the force of political legislation. We are bearers of the gospel message, not of God's will for society.

Our aim, therefore, is not to force people to act like Christians, but to persuade them to consider Christ. Paul reasoned with the Jews in the synagogue, he reasoned with the Greeks and philosophers in the Areopagus, and he almost persuaded King Herod Agrippa II who asked, "Do you think that in such a short time you can persuade me to be a Christian?" To which Paul replied with riveting eloquence, "Short time or long—I pray God that not only you but all who are listening to me today may become what I am, except for these chains" (Acts 26:28-29). We are not here to force our beliefs on society; we are here to argue our faith with such eloquence that those who might be persuaded will have to twist and turn and do loops inside themselves to avoid becoming Christians.

In an address to the World Vision Washington Forum in Seattle in April 1996, Os Guinness lamented the loss of persuasion and apologetics among evangelicals. He also pointed out that this loss is coming at a critical time in history; postmodernism has cleared the table of all the old debates and yet no one seems to have a clue yet how to take advantage of this new opportunity. Guinness feels that there are fewer rivals to the gospel than ever before. Now is the time for a reasoned articulation of our faith that takes into account the intellectual climate of the day and the spiritual hunger of the soul.

Robert D. Richardson's book on the spiritual allusions of Ralph Waldo Emerson has stimulated intellectual discussion of the gospel in an unlikely audience. Richardson expressed surprise at the volume of mail he has received from "people who, if not willing to describe themselves as openly religious, are clearly hungering for a kind of spiritual life that has a serious backing—a seriously respectable intellectual backing that can be believed in by sober people."[3]

Are we ready to take up this discussion? Are we prepared to persuade men and women of the truth? Do we know how to walk among people for whom Christ is not Lord, so that we can reason with them from our hearts where he rules?

3   *No Hope but the Gospel*

A Reason for the Hope

Peter has something specific in mind. "Always be prepared to give an answer to everyone who asks you to give the reason for the hope that you have," is how he puts it. "But do this with gentleness and respect" (1 Pt 3:15).

First, we are to be prepared to give an answer. This implies we stay around long enough and listen hard enough to hear the question. It implies a dialogue. Many of us are not sufficiently engaged in conversation with the world that people will ask us something of such magnitude. To be asked to give a reason for our hope means we've been rubbing shoulders with the world long enough to have our hope show, through our relationships and our work. Now we need to take up the discussion in our own Areopagus, or our faith is of no use in the world.

Peter also tells us to be prepared to give a *reason* for our hope. This means that we have a reasonable hope which will make sense to our generation. To have a reason for our hope is to have a well-thought-out faith that we can articulate in the marketplace of other faiths and ideas. To do this, we need to be carrying on a constant internal dialogue with our faith and our culture. If we are constantly integrating the two in our minds, when someone asks us about our faith, we can continue out loud the conversation that has been going on in our minds all along. Our reason will always be ready.

...with Gentleness and Respect

Although Peter wasn't looking into the 1990s when he wrote this letter, he picked the two words that we need the most... *gentleness* in a time of anger, when the one who shouts the loudest and the last is the one who wins, and *respect* when absolutely no regard is given by anyone, for any position or opinion other than their own.

One mark of postmodernity is that every person is the beginning and the end of his own truth. This is one reason why genteel debate is so rare. Today's debates are not two points of view trying to come closer to the truth or find a better way of solving a problem; they are two truths fighting it out. The encounter yields no synthesis or better understanding of truth, only a winner, a loser, and lots of blood on the battlefield. Of course, both sides usually interpret the results so that they come out on top, as when a candidate loses all the primary delegates but wins "the heart and soul of the party."

Peter's words sound as if they were penned yesterday. "Do not repay evil with evil or insult with insult, but with blessing, because to this you were called so that you may inherit a blessing. For, 'Whoever would love life and see good days must keep his tongue from evil and his lips from deceitful speech. He must turn from evil and do good: he must seek peace and pursue it" (1 Pt 3:9-11).

As Richard Mouw points out in his book *Uncommon Decency*, the society Peter addressed...

was at least as multicultural and pluralistic as ours is today. The early Christians were surrounded by a variety of religious and moral systems. Their pagan neighbors worshiped many gods, and that worship was sometimes so depraved that it would even be shocking in today's permissive culture. What would we think of a religious service in which men were ritually castrated? And the representatives of the dominant culture were not inclined to live and let live when it came to dealing with the early Christian community?

Our forebears in the faith paid dearly for their commitment to the gospel. If they could work at treating people with gentleness and reverence in such an environment, what is our excuse for attempting less?[4]

Christians who believe in a truth outside of their own understanding can contact the world with civility. We can be more gentle and more respectful of those who do not agree with us; we believe truth exists outside of our perceptions and will eventually be found by those who are truly seeking, for God will make himself known. We cannot make anyone see; it is God's work to hide and reveal. We are not out to win, but to bear witness to the truth. We don't have to shout or even have the last word. When we seek to, we are taking a step back from our confidence in the finality of God's truth.

This should be a time in history when Christians frustrate people by *not* fighting. There is no reason to fight. God's truth is true. We are not out to prove anything or to win any ground; we seek to discover more about God and his world. We can even share something with those who are fighting us. As the Apostle Paul tells us, "If your enemy is hungry, feed him; if he is thirsty, give him something to drink... Do not be overcome by evil, but overcome evil with good" (Rom 12:20-21).

One of the ways to overcome evil with good is to respect those we encounter in the world, even if they are antagonistic to the gospel. God has given every human being the choice of seeking him as God or making their own idol to worship. If we are going to respect everyone as made in the image of God, we must respect also their right to believe what they choose. We are not here to crush people, to prove them wrong, or to force them into corners with our superior arguments. We are here to give a reason for our hope to anyone who asks us why we are so hopeful when the world is so hopeless.

Taking It to the Bank

Recently, Senator Mark O. Hatfield, from Oregon, announced his retirement after forty-five years of public service. The news reports that carried the announcement were full of praise for the senator's character and commitment. He was called an iconoclast, a man of principle, a man who stood for what he believed, in spite of the public sway, and a man whose word was reliable. As one reporter put it, "It's common knowledge around Washington that if Mark Hatfield said it, you could take it to the bank."

What wasn't mentioned on the news was the fact that throughout his years of public service, Senator Hatfield has remained a committed Christian. His faith in Jesus Christ has been a quiet and steady strength in his life, something he appears not to have wanted to trumpet as much as live out. At times, his faith has surfaced through his writings and speaking engagements for various Christian institutions or organizations, but he has not chosen to make his Christianity a selling point, a platform, or a means of garnering votes from a certain segment of the population.

Indeed, his personal convictions as a Christian have sometimes clashed with the majority of Christians in the country, particularly when he opposed American involvement in Vietnam and the Persian Gulf. Although his views at times went against his own constituency, the voters of Oregon continued to return him to Congress. That, in itself, is probably the most remarkable tribute to him, that voters wanted to keep him in office for forty-five years, even if they disagreed with some of his policies.

This man represents a kind of Christianity desperately needed today, one that is seen before it is heard. From all appearances, Hatfield is a politician in whose heart Christ is Lord. Because of that lordship, Senator Hatfield has a reputation as a public official who can be trusted—a man of his word—certainly a rare commodity among politicians today.

When it comes to his faith, Mark Hatfield has chosen to keep his words few, and to adopt a sleeves-rolled-up approach to being a public servant. As he comes to the end of his political career, the accolades to his character the longer of which include mention of his faith, are a strong witness to his faith in Christ.

But, did Senator Hatfield miss the chance to use his platform for the gospel? I would contend that, by being the kind of man and politician that he was, he performed an even greater service for the gospel than if he were drawing attention to it every other day. His manner of being faithful to his calling as a Christian was to be a great senator. He was not known for being a Christian, but for being a fair-minded, trustworthy, principled, hardworking peacemaker in public service, and when all is said and done, what's the difference? We need more Christians who are known for being outstanding people in whose hearts Christ is Lord.

This is the crux of Peter's message in his letter to the postmodern church. Our reputation in the world gives credibility to what we say. Our contribution to society quiets any opposition. Our hope begs the question. Our attitude toward non-Christians gives us the opportunity to speak, "...keeping a clear conscience, so that those who speak maliciously against your good behavior in

Christ may be ashamed of their slander" (1 Pt 3:16).

Wouldn't it be a switch if people wanted to put us down for our faith but couldn't, because we were doing so much good in the community that to put us down would make *them* look bad? Unfortunately, some Christians in the public eye of late have given more reason *for* slander than reason to refute it. Peter is talking about a life that acts out faith in love and good deeds, so that when something *is* said about Christ, it comes at the request of those who have noticed a quality worth investigating.

5   *Conclusion*

Another Letter to Scattered Strangers

The prophet Jeremiah wrote a letter to people in a similar situation as the first century church and our postmodern church today. It was a letter sent "from Jerusalem to the surviving elders among the exiles and to the priests, the prophets and all the other people Nebuchadnezzar had carried into exile from Jerusalem to Babylon" (Jer 29:1). The parallels are obvious. America is not Jerusalem but is much closer to Babylon by nature. The children of Israel were not in captivity to call Babylon back to God. Babylon never belonged to God in the way Israel did. No other nation ever has or ever will. Israel was in captivity because the people were disobedient, and yet God remained faithful to them. And while they were there, certain accommodations with Babylon were necessary. Though not serving allegiance to Babylon, they nevertheless interacted with its culture and its life. Jeremiah's instructions to them are surprisingly relevant to us today as strangers, scattered throughout this postmodern age in our American Babylon.

This is what the Lord Almighty, the God of Israel, says to all those carried into exile from Jerusalem to Babylon: "Build houses and settle down; plant gardens and eat what they produce. Marry and have sons and daughters; find wives for your sons and give your daughters in marriage, so that they too may have sons and daughters. Increase in number there; do not decrease. Also, seek the peace and prosperity of the city to which I have carried you into exile. Pray to the Lord for it, because if it prospers, you too will prosper." Yes, this is what the Lord Almighty, the God of Israel, says: "Do not let the prophets and diviners among you deceive you. Do not listen to the dreams you encourage them to have. They are prophesying lies to you in my name. I have not sent them," declares the Lord.   JEREMIAH 29:4-7

Just as in the days of Jeremiah and Peter, so there will be plenty of prophets and preachers eager to feed us the dreams we want to hear. Some will tell us we are not in exile after all, that our Babylon is really Jerusalem and we are going to rule it. Don't listen to them. There is only one rule we are to concern ourselves with and that is the rule of the Lord Jesus Christ over our hearts and minds.

But neither are we to be antagonistic toward our Babylon. We are to pray for it and contribute to its peace and prosperity; for though it is not the kingdom of God, it allows the kingdom of God to exist and even flourish within its boundaries, thus spreading far and wide the good news of God's grace to all who are coming to faith.

POSTSCRIPT

Out, Not *Up*

It is not in the interest of spreading the gospel that God's people be a sequestered ethnic group any longer. The great message of the gospel is intended to go to the ends of the earth. To accomplish that, the people of God must be found in all cultures, eating and drinking, enjoying music and art, and making tools with those who do not yet know the gospel.[1]
KENNETH A. MYERS

"The kingdom of heaven is like a mustard seed, which a man took and planted in his field. Though it is the smallest of all your seeds, yet when it grows, it is the largest of garden plants and becomes a tree, so that the birds of the air come and perch in its branches" (Mt 13:31-32).

This parable of Jesus is usually interpreted as the growth of the gospel message which becomes a resting place and a security for the believer. Indeed, some today see it as being fulfilled in the growth and power of the Christian infrastructure that witnesses for Christ in the world by drawing attention to itself and allowing believers to be protected under its growing influence.

But there is one problem with this interpretation. The plant Jesus is most likely referring to is commonly known as a shrub. Though it has been reported to have reached a height of ten feet, hardly a tree with "big branches" (Mk 4:32), its average height is only four feet.

A controversial interpretation, but worthy of consideration, is that this parable predicts abnormal growth in the kingdom of God. It is not inconsistent with the parables to have evil influences enter into what Jesus terms "the kingdom of heaven." He uses the same words, "The kingdom of heaven is like..." to introduce the tares sown with the wheat (see Mt 13:24-30) and the leaven which contaminates the whole loaf (v. 33).

The same image of a tree that protects birds in its branches is used to picture the evil kingdoms of Assyria (see Ez 31:2-14) and

Babylon (see Dn 4:10-15), both trees which God felled with a mighty blow. And only a few verses prior to this parable is the parable of the sower, where the birds that came and ate the seeds sown on the road represented the evil one snatching the Word of God away. Could this tree be where these birds go when they are not snatching up seeds in the marketplace?

If this is one way the Savior warns us about a tendency in his kingdom toward a false security and an abnormal influence in the world, it might also suggest how he desires his gospel to be spread. For the normal growth of the mustard plant is not *up* as much as it is *out*, as it spreads its influence out across the hillsides, scattering its seed in the wind.

Regardless of the proper interpretation of this parable, the picture of Christians as a quiet, steady invasion of mustard seeds carried on the wind of the Spirit and taking root among the tares of the world—spreading our influence wherever we land as a fragrance to God and a benefit to man—is a good picture of how we are to live in the world.

We know that evil can perch in the superstructure of modern Christianity. We know that where money and power and glory are, there will also be mixed motives and deception. We know that the church is not to be a city of refuge away from the perturbations of the world, but a growing, vulnerable, living organism with wide-reaching influence on the world and its cultures.

Pascal captured the paradox of both the frailty and the brilliance of our human existence by calling man "a thinking reed." A thinking mustard plant would seem a fitting picture for a Christian in the world.

Out is the operative word for us in the world. Out from the comforts and securities of a defined subculture into the challenges of a world filled with the relentless choice between good and evil, between the true God and replicas of him we erect in our holy places. *Out* into a world waiting for the gospel and its messengers; *up* is only another Babel. There will be no *up* for Christians until we are all escorted there by the returning victorious Christ.

> Good will come to him who is generous and lends freely,
>   who conducts his affairs with justice.
> Surely he will never be shaken;
>   a righteous man will be remembered forever.
> He will have no fear of bad news;
>   his heart is steadfast, trusting in the Lord.
> His heart is secure, he will have no fear;
>   in the end he will look in triumph on his foes.
> He has scattered abroad his gifts to the poor,
>   his righteousness endures forever;
>   his horn will be lifted high in honor.   Psalms 112:5-9

Notes

ONE
Two Worlds

1. Isaac Watts, "Am I a Soldier of the Cross?"
2. Harry Blamires, *The Christian Mind* (Ann Arbor, Mich.: Servant, 1963), 3.
3. Blamires, 27.
4. C.S. Lewis, *The Voyage of the Dawn Treader* (New York: Macmillan, 1952), 143.
5. *USA Today*, 20 February 1996.
6. Blamires, 27.
7. Sandra Dallas, "Onward Christian Publishers," *Business Week*, 31 July 1995, 44.
8. Dallas, 44.
9. Michael S. Horton, *Beyond Culture Wars* (Chicago: Moody, 1994), 132.
10. Mark Noll, *The Scandal of the Evangelical Mind* (Grand Rapids, Mich.: Eerdmans, 1994), 7.

TWO
Thinking Someone Else's Thoughts

1. Lewis, 140.
2. From an address by Os Guinness at the World Vision Washington Forum in Seattle, April 1996.
3. Robert W. Jenson, Mars Hill Tapes, #20, March/April 1996. Readers will notice a number of quotes from Mars Hill Tapes, a bimonthly audio magazine of contemporary culture and Christian conviction. These are ninety minute cassette-taped interviews with current authors and thinkers narrated by Ken Myers. Any Mars Hill Tape would yield numerous quotes for this book as they are always relevant to contemporary issues. I know of no other publication doing this necessary integration of faith and culture and I highly recommend a subscription for the thinking Christian. For more information and/or a free demo tape contact: P.O. Box 1527 Charlottesville, VA 22902-1527, or 1-800-331-6407.
4. Kenneth A. Myers, Mars Hill Tapes, #18, November/December, 1995.
5. See Russell B. Goodman, *Pragmatism: A Contemporary Reader* (New York: Routledge, 1995).
6. Paul Edwards, ed., *The Encyclopedia of Philosophy*, (New York: Macmillan, 1972), 435.

7. Marcus G. Singer, "Pragmatism" *The World Book Encyclopedia* (Chicago: World Book, 1984), v.15, 655.

8. Avrum Stoll, Richard Popkin, *Introduction to Philosophy,* (New York: Holt, Rinehart & Winston, 1961), 364.

9. See John Patrick Diggins, *The Promise of Pragmatism* (Chicago: University of Chicago Press, 1995) for a discussion of postmodern pragmatism.

10. Rodney Clapp, "The Sin of Winnie-the-Pooh," *Christianity Today,* 9 November 1992, v36, n13, 29.

11. *The Harvard Classics,* Volume 48 (New York: P.F. Collier and Son, 1959), 99.

12. Robert Farrar Capon, "The Astonished Heart," *The Bell Lecture,* 23 October 1994.

13. Peter Kreeft, *The Best Things in Life* (Downers Grove, Ill.: InterVarsity Press, 1984), 20.

14. T. S. Eliot, *The Collected Poems and Plays* (New York: Harcourt, Brace & World, 1971), 232.

15. Kreeft, 31.

16. Charles Sykes, *Mars Hill Tapes,* #19, January/February 1996, Charlottesville, VA.

17. Dorothy L. Sayers, *A Matter of Eternity,* (Grand Rapids, Mich.: Eerdmans, 1973), 114.

18. Sayers, 135.

19. Quoted from a Doonesbury cartoon by Garry Trudeau.

20. *Statistical Abstract of the United States,* (Washington, D.C.: U.S. Bureau of the Census), 189.

21. Studs Terkel, *The Great Divide* (New York: Pantheon Books, 1988), 27.

22. Terkel, 28.

THREE
Whose World?

1. Ron Sider, "On Bibles and Ballots," *Prism,* May/June 1996, v3, n4, 13.

2. Sider, 5.

3. James Fallows, "Why Americans Hate the Media" *Atlantic Monthly,* February 1996, v277, v2, 55.

4. Fallows, 52.

5. *The New York Times,* 11 March 1995.

6. Pete Hamill, "End Game," *Esquire,* December 1994, 85.

7. Blaise Pascal, *Thoughts and Minor Works* (New York: P.F. Collier & Son, 1959), 192.

8. Frederick Buechner, *Telling the Truth* (New York: Harper & Row, 1977), 89.

9. Mars Hill Tapes, #20, March/April 1996.

10. Readers interested in getting involved in environmental concerns might want to con-

tact Christian Environmental Association, 1650 Zanker Road, Suite 150, San Jose, CA 95112; 408/441-1571. For $100 you can purchase an acre of rain forest next to a national park in Belize, Central America and save it from destruction. There are also numerous short term service projects available through C.E.A.'s Target Earth program for those interested in hands-on involvement.

11.   Horton, 78.

12.   Isaac Watts, *I Sing the Mighty Power of God.*

FOUR
One World

1.   Quoted by Richard Mouw, *Uncommon Decency* (Downer's Grove: InterVarsity Press, 1992), 147.

2.   *Esquire,* April 1996.

3.   Screwtape is a demon in C.S. Lewis's *Screwtape Letters* who terrorizes Christians often by misusing good things and making the good the enemy of the best.

4.   Ranald Macaulay and Jerram Barrs, *Being Human* (Downers Grove, Ill.: InterVarsity Press, 1978), 39.

5.   Macaulay and Barrs, 39.

6.   Macaulay and Barrs, 55.

7.   Rod Beaton, "Behind the Seams," *USA Today,* 31 May 1996, 4C.

8.   Brennan Manning, *Abba's Child* (Colorado Springs: NavPress, 1994), 48.

9.   Brother Lawrence, *The Practice of the Presence of God* (Springdale, Penn.: Whitaker House, 1982), 4.

10.   Brother Lawrence, 20.

11.   Brother Lawrence, 20.

12.   Maltbie D. Babcock, *This Is My's Father's World.*

FIVE
Finding the Unknown God

1.   Kenneth A. Myers, *All God's Children and Blue Suede Shoes,* (Wheaton, Ill.: Crossway, 1989), 87.

2.   Horton, 34.

3.   Steve Turner, *Hungry for Heaven* (Downers Grove, Ill.: InterVarsity Press, 1995), 218.

4.   Robert Farrar Capon, *The Bell Lecture,* "The Astonished Heart," 23 October 1994.

SIX
Saints Too Soon

1. Manning, 82.
2. Manning, 87.
3. C.S. Lewis, *Screwtape Letters* (New York: Macmillan, 1943), 85.
4. Lewis, *Screwtape Letters*, 86.
5. Elizabeth C. Clephan, "Beneath the Cross of Jesus".

SEVEN
Letter to the Postmodern Church

1. Richard Mouw, *Uncommon Decency* (Downers Grove, Ill.: InterVarsity, 1992), 13.
2. John Seel, *No God But God: Breaking with the Idols of Our Age, Mars Hill Reports*, MHR-1, by Foundation Focus.
3. *Now or Never: How We Can Save Our Public Schools*, (Dallas: Taylor, 1995).
4. These criteria are spelled out more fully in information that can be obtained from Leadership Network. For more information on social entrepreneurs or for assistance in identifying with them, contact Fred Smith at 1-800-765-5323.
5. "Viewpoints," *The Dallas Morning News*, 21 April 1996.
6. Cheryl M. Bacon, "Into the Gap," *ACU Today*, Abilene Christian University Magazine, Winter 1995.

EIGHT
A Reason for the Hope

1. Turner, 159.
2. Robert W. Jenson, Mars Hill Tapes, #20, March/April 1996.
3. Robert D. Richardson, Mars Hill Tapes, #20, March/April 1996.
4. Mouw, 17.

POSTSCRIPT

1. Myers, 49.

ABOUT THE AUTHOR

John Fischer has been on the cutting edge of contemporary Christian culture, both as a recording artist and author, for over two decades. An award-winning columnist for *Contemporary Christian Music* magazine, he is the author of nine books including *Real Christians Don't Dance*, *Saint Ben*, *Be Thou My Vision*, and *On a Hill Too Far Away*.

OTHER BOOKS OF INTEREST
FROM JOHN FISCHER

Be Thou My Vision
Daily Inspiration from the Greatest Hymns of All Time
John Fischer

For centuries, hymns of beauty and timeless truth have helped to kindle the fire of faith in believers' hearts. Now Christians can fan the flame in their own lives with these daily reflections on sacred themes.

Be Thou My Vision offers eloquent reminders of the character of God and the wonders of creation. Whether these glorious hymns represent uncharted territory for you or familiar buoys in the midst of a deep and treacherous ocean, you will find within these pages a place to cast a line and anchor to the truth.

ISBN 0-89283-924-4, Trade paper, $12.99

On a Hill Too Far Away
Getting the Cross Back in the Center of Our Lives
John Fischer

In this passionate book, John Fischer prompts us to recall what our hearts once knew: the cross is our only hope. It has changed history— and us—forever. *On a Hill Too Far Away* rekindles our desire and longing for the cross, restores our vision of the incredible grace which transforms our lives and reshapes our culture, and calls us to remember the most spectacular truth of all: incredible Sundays always follow Good Fridays.

ISBN: 0-89283-839-6, Trade paper, $10.99

Available at your Christian bookstore or from:
Servant Publications
Dept. 209
P.O. Box 7455
Ann Arbor, Michigan 48107
Please include payment plus $2.75 per book for postage and handling.